BULLE

ALPHA MALE

Build Mental Toughness and Become a Real Alpha Male. Self-Discipline Stratagems to Increase your Confidence and Self-Esteem, Enhance your Charisma and Reach your Goals

Kingsley Register

Table of Contents

Introduction

An Alpha Male is a man who has no problems being himself. It may sound effortless, and we may even think that it's easy to be ourselves all the time, but the truth is, but it isn't. If it was, then why are there many men uncomfortable with themselves? The fact that you're reading this book probably means that you, too, are having a difficult time being comfortable in your skin.

Another characteristic of alpha males is passion, which simply means love for what they're doing. This isn't the kind of love that society, your friends, and your family may necessarily encourage you to have. It's all about what you truly and personally care for and love. It's about your core being.

An example of this would be 'writing.' My mom and most of my friends look down on my choice of trading my corporate (hell) job for freelance writing, which I genuinely love. The truth is that hand has made me come alive in ways that my old corporate job never did. My corporate job killed the real me in many ways! And this was despite a more significant and steadier paycheck!

Alpha males act differently from the rest of the human pack because they see things differently. For example, while most other males—omega ones probably—see life as one big people-pleasing party, alpha males see it in another way. While most people believe that being bashful and courteous—only in terms of letting others have their way—is the way to earning people's respect and favor, alpha males believe that such an approach is akin to suicide and that they need to confidently assert themselves.

For the alpha male, optimism is what holds things together, which other males don't see. Alpha males are generally optimistic, particularly about themselves. They look at themselves in the mirror and see their bright future ahead of them. They don't see constraints and threats. It's why they push people to speak cleverer, faster, and better than they do. It's why they don't stop giving others chances. And it's why they don't give up.

The alpha male doesn't give up.

The alpha male doesn't take shit from others either. Not for any reason. Not because of societal expectations and pressure tactics. Not because he is ignorant of the life—he is indeed leading. He knows what he is doing. And he does it with authority, conviction, and strength.

Even when the alpha male is wrong, he is right.

Because stubbornness is his game, he will not be swayed by what others think, say, and do.

That's the alpha male; a man who isn't swayed by most other people at all, ever.

Are you ready to be an alpha male?

Are you ready to go your own way?

Are you ready to come alive?

Am I getting you all fired up and pumped up to be an alpha male? Good! That's the way I want you to be too—ready and set to be what you want to be. Don't settle for less. Don't pay attention to others' expectations.

Take hold of your destiny, because it's there for taking—and it's all up to you.

For example, you are now reading a book about becoming an alpha male. Bravo! You've taken the first step. That's where the buck stops. Accept responsibility for life in its entirety. Start now! Don't wait!

Yes, you'll have a "beta" tag for at least a while. You'll have an "omega" tag. You may even be tagged as "gamma," "delta" or worse. But don't fret over it, because that's exactly what everyone expects from you now. That's what they know you for. You're a person who places a premium on appearances and external influences—not on personal growth.

As you're reading, you're probably thinking that the concept of being an alpha male would be something you would find in a science fiction movie or the world of "The Lord of the Rings." While alpha males are not ordinary, as you may know, you may find them in the most ordinary places.

You fall in love with and see a person who thinks and acts differently than you; that's alpha status; that's alpha romantic love.

Alpha males strive to be independent, assertive, and confident. And they don't give a damn about what anybody else thinks. They are the exact opposite of you—who keeps seeking validation from others. Whom you keep trying to please. Whom you keep trying to prove something to. Whom you keep begging to accept you and your love—it's not going to work.

But to up the ante, I want you to strive to be even more independent from others, more confident and assertive, and even more profound.

What's stopping you? Your fear? Your emotions? Your societal conditioning? Your friends? Your family?

4

Nonetheless, if you were the person who knew the truth; you'd act differently; You'd be in control.

You claim to know the truth—the way you see the world. And you claim to love yourself. But are you truly doing that?

If you were truly honest with yourself about who you are at the core, you'd realize that the answer is a resounding NO! You're not honest with yourself. And that's why you keep trying to impress others and even fool them.

Being honest with yourself is about being ready to be yourself to make an exception for yourself.

If you're not honest with yourself, be honest right now.

Are you ready to be yourself?

Alpha males lead by example. They are the legends that we all aspire to be.

Are you ready to stand out, be considered a legend in your own terms, and lead others with your example?

How about that? You are following that thread of thought to be more than you thought you would. It is perfect. I like it.

Now, what are you working on? You may already be doing it. You may already be channeling the alpha male. It's in you somewhere. Are you listening to yourself? Do you know what you want? Even if you don't, your own words will. They will speak your right and good feelings.

Align yourself with your sense of self-respect. This is where your real strength lies.

You already have the answers to what you want. You want to be the alpha male.

Chapter 1: The Signs That Sabotage Your Success in Being an Alpha Male

Being an "alpha" is not sexually oriented. It's a unisex title as the two sexual orientations take a beautiful high position of intensity in the labor force and business world. Alphas are the individuals who run the world—so they are called alphas—which implies first and best in class.

It's not just about being smooth or steaming Moxy, and there is significantly more that goes into carrying on with the alpha way of life than numerous lone fantasies about sex. It's tied in with carrying on with a day-to-day existence brimming with satisfaction and self-completion. The alpha lifestyle lives inside us all. However, it must be acknowledged, or, more than likely, it stays inside until the end of time.

To be effective, you need to have your alpha character sparkle. Infrequently, throughout humankind's entire existence, there has been a beta that has dominated other people.

Our skills and capacities make for a division in life, some individuals give orders and some others take them. The alphas order from a place of intensity that is moved by their certainty and capacity to control and move others. Here are the attributes of your alpha character that you need to develop.

The Alpha Male Is Determined: There's no stopping in this individual. He's the turtle, not the rabbit—the sole survivor. Diligence will get you all over; it's tied in with getting farther than every other person.

The Alpha Male Is Specific: He can stroll into a room without knowing anybody and still be the bubbling energy source that everyone crowds around and the focal point of consideration. The certainty pushes him to do so.

The Alpha Male Is Fit as a Fiddle: Nobody needs to see a fat fellow or somebody in his 30s who resembles susceptibility to a treadmill. It's tied in with being dependable and looking tasteful, satisfying to everybody around him.

The Alpha Male Is Bold: He doesn't need dread. Instead, he acknowledges that it exists and faces it at each chance. He comprehends that in this world, you need to have the courage to get something going.

The Alpha Male Can Engage: His comical inclination can have a gathering of individuals listening to all his words. It's tied in with talking with sureness and having individuals eating out of your hands.

The Alpha Male Has Stories to Tell: He has lived—and is living—a one-of-a-kind life. He has committed errors; however, he can discover humor in them. He has had experiences that everybody needs to catch wind off. He carries on with his life when others don't approach him.

The Alpha Male Can Snicker at Himself: This is, for the most part, an over-looked trademark, yet an important one. The alpha man can't be ridiculed, because he participates and nobody can show better improvements than him.

The Alpha Male Is Unassuming: Regardless of how far he gets throughout everyday life, regardless of how well off he is, the alpha mas is grounded and always remembers where he came from. He has seen the battle and the excursion and has been humbled by it.

The Alpha Male Has knowledge: A degree is anything but essential, yet a pang of hunger for information is. He learns continuously and has good common sense. This causes him to understand everything and everybody with whom he comes in contact. He can take a discussion anyplace from French wine to motors and football.

The Alpha Male Is Amazingly Amiable: He is intense, regularly tranquil, formed, and has poise, yet can transform anything into a decent time.

The Alpha Male Makes His Words Important: He doesn't talk just to hear the sound of his voice. His words are picked cautiously. He regards the intensity of words and realizes how to evoke precisely what he wants from them.

The Alpha Male Has a Reason: This might be his most characterizing quality. Where others are just attempting to know themselves through the meanders of life, the alpha man is too occupied with making himself. Consistently, he plans something to carry himself closer to his objective. He doesn't wander carelessly and burns through his time. He understands what he needs, and he knows how he will get it.

The Alpha Male Is a Diligent Employee: He realizes that nothing incredible is cultivated without difficult work and a positive reason. He isn't the person who runs out of the workplace at 5 pm and stops his email.

The Alpha Male Is an Individual of Significant Worth: "Do whatever it takes not to turn into a man of accomplishment, but instead attempt to turn into a man of significant worth." Einstein realized that achievement is accomplished through valuation. The alpha is a man of significant worth and qualities. He improves the lives of others by being a piece of them.

The Alpha Male Helps Other People: He is liberal and gets satisfaction out of fulfilling others. Life isn't just about achievements, but additionally about leaving a legacy. That legacy is how he caused others to feel and how he helps other people achieve their dreams.

The Alpha Male Is a Pioneer: He shows others how it's done. He doesn't advise individuals how to live, yet lives in the way he sees as best—and individuals follow him for it.

Alpha Males Since Forever: Achilles, William Wallace, and Napoleon saw opportunity where others saw disappointment. The alpha will fizzle; however, he won't consider an inability to be the end. He considers it to be a vital piece of the experience—a venturing stone. Realizing this permits him to attempt things others won't, and work more diligently when others typically quit—betas run from disappointment.

The Alpha Male Is Obstinate: His hardheadedness is the thing that will make him the best individual he needs to be. At the point when he begins something he is energetic about, nobody can hold him up. He is into it until the end. He is confident and objective, and consequently, he succeeds. It is tied in with having no self-question and following what you need.

The Alpha Male Doesn't Attempt to Be an Alpha Male: That is the place where so many fall flat. He is keen on life and on living. He's interested in his general surroundings and in turning into the best man he can turn into. He often thinks about others.

He buckles down energetically. He's energized by life, and by the open door that every day presents. He's real in each aspect of what his identity is. All of these attributes are usually controlled by him or will be as he develops as a man. Reproduced from interest, an authentic generosity, and a hero's heart, he is the kind of person he is, and all others follow him any place he will lead them to.

Chapter 2: The Science and Psychology Behind the Alpha Male

Have you seen the "smash or pass" game on YouTube? If not, it's straightforward. The video host approaches a girl or a group of girls, shows them pictures of guys, and asks them, "Smash or pass?"

Does smash or pass mean that you would sleep with this guy based solely on what you see in the picture?

EVERYONE is playing the smash or pass game in their head, all day, every day.

You play it all the time. Every time you see a woman and your mind says, "damn..." That means to smash. When you see bootydoo, pass.

And how long does it take to make that decision? About 2 seconds. The time it takes for your eyes to give her a quick up-and-down, a decision is made.

Does this sound familiar?

Does this sound like the thought experiment we performed earlier in Make Women Chase You? The one with the ten women bald vs. dressed for the club.

And what did we determine at the end of that experiment? That what you look like IS essential. But what you look like has little to do with your facial bone structure and everything to do with variables within your control.

Well, women are playing the smash or pass game too, All day, every day. They are indeed playing it with men who approach them with sexual interest.

So, here's how the game works out in real life:

A smash decision means that based on what you look like—again, almost entirely within your control—and you are a potential sex partner. That doesn't mean she's going to have sex with you. It just means that you're not immediately and permanently dismissed. That's the first hurdle.

A pass decision means you're immediately and permanently dismissed. Once this happens, she might still talk to you for a minute, but it's pretty much over.

To get a smash decision, we need to take charge of all the variables we can control.

Always Be Ready: If keeping yourself fresh and groomed regularly isn't a habit, you need to make it a habit immediately. If you don't, it's effortless to let hot women walk away by using the excuse, "I wasn't ready." That's a bullshit excuse.

Starting today, you need always to be ready. Leave the house every day to approach women. And being groomed and prepared to come even if you're going out to run errands.

This doesn't mean you have to approach every woman you see. It just means you'll be ready when a hottie appears right in front of you. Because for some reason, 'hotties' always seem to appear when you're 'not ready.' So, from now on, always be 'ready.'

Hair: Have a fresh, crisp haircut. Ideally, one that best fits your face. There are tons of information out there to help you with this. "Google" this topic or find a good barber and have them figure it out. Believe me that a good haircut can dramatically impact what you look like. At a minimum, just make sure you have a fresh trim.

Beard: If you're going to shave, be freshly shaved. If you look good with a 5 o'clock shadow, take advantage of that. I know lots of guys that rock the 5 o'clock. Here's the key: Make sure the 5 o'clock looks intentional—not like you were just lazy and didn't shave. How? Shave all around the edges of your 5 o'clock. Shave off the bottom ½ inch of the neckline, so there is a crisp line

15

separating the 5 o'clock from the rest of your neck. Shave the lines on the cheek, so they are crispy. Shave any stragglers at the top of your mustache—just under the nose. A good hairstyle can look great—as long as they look like you did it on purpose.

If you rock a beard, take some time to learn about grooming styles. How you groom your beard can have a dramatic impact on what you look like. You can groom yourself to make your chin look more prominent. How? Here are the basics:

Think of your beard in 3 areas: The goatee (area a), the sideburns straight down to the jaw (area c), and the space in between those two (area b). Let's say your razor has three shaving lengths from 1 to 3, with three being the longest. You start by shaving your entire beard with a 3 (the longest). Then you shave everything except the goatee (area a) using a 2 (the middle length). Then you shave the sideburns area (area c) with a 1 (the shortest distance).

This makes your beard fade from short to middle to long as you look from ear to chin. That creates the illusion of you having a longer, more pronounced jaw and chin.

And last, but not less important, shave any visible hair off your nose and ears.

Fingernails: They should be short and clean under the nail.

The Fragrance: You should be showered, clean, and deodorized. Hit yourself with two squirts of expensive cologne. I like one spray on the upper body and a second on the crotch because, who knows, that double rush could be useful some day.

Poor Man's Hack: If you're a broke college dude, swing by the mall before any hot date, go to the fragrance area in a department store, and hit yourself with the samples.

Oral Hygiene: Brush your teeth. Pop a tic-tac. A lot of people find that chewing gum just makes them feel more confident. It's a strange phenomenon. Try it out. Plus, women always ask if they can have a piece of gum. You can give them, but only with conditions that they do something for you (more on handling tests coming up soon).

Clothes: This is where a lot of guys get hung up—a fashion advice can be a book in and of itself, and what looks good will be different for everybody. So, let's keep it simple.

The best fashion for you is clean, crisp, fresh-looking clothes that you are comfortable in. Whatever you can wear that makes you feel the most confident is the best choice for now.

In general, stick to solid neutral colors. Don't be too 'loud' with your clothes unless you are intentionally peacocking.

Differentiator: You should have between 1 and 3 unique differentiators. These are generally watches, bracelets, necklaces, rings, and earrings. The choice and style will vary depending on your personality and what makes you feel comfortable. But trust me, I've seen guys with ears full of rings having women falling all over them. So, anything can work when you make it work.

Ideally, any differentiator should have a little story associated with it. Or it should have some meaning or significance to you—as you got it on some trip, or someone important gave it to you. This is because a differentiator is a common thing to initiate an initial conversation with a woman. She will notice it, might point it out, and ask about it. So, have something to say about it.

If you literally can't think of anything to say about your differentiator, you can just tell her, "Cuz it looks good" (confident wink, confident smirk).

Don't overlook the differentiator. Get at least one. It's essential to make you subtly stand out from the crowd.

Body language - The Basics

When You're Walking: Walk with intention and purpose—saunter. Don't scurry like a little mouse. Walk around like you own the place. Walk into a room like you own the business. Walk around like you're the worst ass motherfucker in the world.

Because in your world, you are the worst motherfucker. So, act like it.

When You Sit: Open up and uncross your legs. Uncross your arms. Take up more space. Sit in a way that takes up as much space as possible.

When You Stand: Open your legs, straighten your back and hold your head high. Hands out of your pockets—or if in your pockets, thumbs out. Don't put your entire hand in your pocket.

Eye Movements: They should be slow and intentional. Keep your eyes from flickering and fluttering. Make intense eye contact with women. This doesn't mean staring. It means if you make eye contact with a woman, look at her like a fucking man. Don't let your eyes pull away because you're scared. Look at her like you know everything she could say. Look at her like you're the keeper of her soul.

Head Movements: They should be slow and intentional. You don't need to head bobble in agreement with everything people say. Just look at them with a smirk.

Slow Down Everything You Do: Slow down. Talk slower. Walk slower. Chew slower. Put your fork down on the table between bites. Turn your head to look at things more deliberately. Answer slower. Pause for dramatic effect.

Have a Deep Voice: To this one, you may be saying that you can't change your voice and that you can't make yourself have a deep voice, because people try that and hurt their vocal cords. Well, here's the secret of a deep voice: Slow down. That's it. Slow your talking down. The faster you talk, the more your voice will uncontrollably rise in pitch. So, slow it down.

All of the grooming items above are critical from day 1. So, read the list over if necessary and get these things in order.

For body language, start by improving one thing. If it's walking with slow intention and purpose—walking like you own the place—then consciously practice improving that everywhere you go. Spend a week on it. Do it until it feels natural. Then pick something else. Focus some energy on these things, and you will master them. Then it will be natural, and you won't need to think about doing it.

Chapter 3: Learn the Art of Detachment

On the off chance that you need to be the sort of fellow that a top-notch lady finds overwhelming at that point, you must get familiar with the craft of separation. However long you go about as though it doesn't make a difference, if you come up short or not, you won't fizzle since you will have a good time.

Being segregated in this setting has a few implications.

Initially, you should figure out how to give a lady her space when you're connecting with her. As both of you become more acquainted with each other and turn out to be more private later on—there will be a lot of time for being close and near inseparable as a couple. Be that as it may, for the present moment, give her some space.

That tells her that you're not an impoverished person who's frantically searching for a sweetheart. Ladies can smell edginess well in advance, and they quickly run the other way.

Furthermore, as you connect with her, keep up the mood that while you'd love for her to like you, you're not hell-bent on attempting to make her like you. Have a confident, triumphant demeanor that imparts that you know you're an incredible person and that you don't need to demonstrate it to anybody. Be laid back and benevolent, and go about as though nothing else matters except for the occasion.

This is the thing that individuals genuinely mean when they state somebody is cool. 'Cool' individuals are just separated from it all. They don't mind in any case. Even though they do not put many resources into getting the results, they are keener on getting a charge out, existing apart from everything else, and guaranteeing that everybody will have good memories of them.

You're not considering, on the off chance, that she'll need to see you again, or in case you will say something dumb. You just couldn't care less. You're not reasoning if you should call first or if she'll call you since you basically couldn't care less about the result. The only thing you care about is the occasion, how it feels to be around her, and whether she's fascinating to you. Just feed off of that energy and let it impact your connection with her.

The more segregated you are from a circumstance, the more unmistakably you can think, and the more connected with it you'd be at the time. Investing an excessive amount of energy pondering future outcomes is the surest method of disappointment in everyday issues. Center around the second and feel sure that things will consistently work out.

Embrace this demeanor, or use it as self-talk at whatever point you feel as though you're making a decent attempt or that you may fizzle. You just say to yourself:

"It doesn't make a difference if she prefers me or not. I like myself a great deal, which is the only important thing since I regard myself, and individuals like me because they regard me. Moreover, I believe I'm a beautiful and cool individual, and I possibly need to know whether she's a lovely cool individual too. On the off chance that she doesn't wind up loving me, that is fine—also, if she winds up loving me, that is fine too. Not being preferred has never murdered anybody. In this way, whatever occurs, I'm alright with it, and it truly doesn't make a difference to me whichever way since I'm certainly going to make some great memories regardless."

Focus on having as much fun as humanly conceivable in any social circumstance, and you will have revealed an undiscovered wellspring of fortunate force. I recommend that you compose that little self-chat on a significant piece of paper and stick it up somewhere you can peruse it consistently. Even better, compose that on a card and keep it in your pocket or your wallet and carry it around with you. Peruse it just before you interact with any lady and use it as your "coolness credo." It will be precious to you if you do it as it will help you a great deal when associating with ladies.

You should allow it to turn into your way of thinking while interacting with ladies, but also with anybody all in all. It's an extraordinary method to take a gander at the world since you'll never require the endorsement of others to appreciate your worth.

Trust me, on the off chance that you read this book, and this is the solitary internal game strategy that you ace, you'll be a lot more joyful in your connections. Dominating this part of the inward game will make it simpler for a decent lady to like you— predominantly because you'll be the sort of man who doesn't allow things to get to him so effectively... including her.

At the point when a lady understands that she isn't the sole integral factor in your genuine feelings of serenity, she will turn out to be absurdly intrigued and pulled into you. She'll need to understand what matters to you, what your considerations are, and how you carry on with your life. By being withdrawn, you wind up succeeding nearly because you didn't overthink a lot.

It resembles that you consider accomplishment to be inescapable to you. You consider it a position of wealth. Furthermore, because you both accept and act like achievement is inescapable, the achievement will ultimately turn into your existence. This is the reason why the less you stress over progress, the simpler it will be for you.

It's an 'odd oddity,' yet it's one that works. So, make sure to utilize it for your potential benefit.

Chapter 4: Build the Atomic Charisma

Alpha guys overflow with allure; they're attractive and enchanting. Be that as it may, don't think, "you've either got it, or you don't." While a few people are generally magnetic, it's a quality you can develop through training—and the capacity to be appealing has nothing to do with your race, sexual orientation, character, or being a loner or social butterfly. There is an assortment of hidden social abilities that you can use to be that magnetic alpha male.

Here are methods upheld by science:

Talk with Your Hands

Alpha guys are profoundly lucid. If you talk and impart utilizing your hands, you'll be seen as more dependable and engaging, as indicated by tests done. One of the principal zones you usually see when meeting another person is their hands. Evolutionists clarify, it was significant for human endurance in our "agrarian" days to ensure others were not conveying any weapons.

Demonstrating your palms defuses the subliminal security component and passes on you as non-threatening to other people.

Individuals will be more attracted to you once they feel great with you. What's more, utilizing hand signals additionally causes you to convey better. It's designated "typified insight," which means there's a significant association between the thing your brain is attempting to measure and state and your body developments. Moving your hands assists your brain with passing on your musings.

So, whenever you're having a discussion, be deliberate about utilizing your hands—you'll be more well-spoken and alluring.

Utilize Her Name

The most effective method to be beguiling.

Alpha guys are connecting with and consistently utilize an individual's name when addressing them. Researchers utilizing fMRI found that particular pieces of the cerebrum were enacted when individuals heard their name. It causes them to feel vast and esteemed.

When somebody acquaints themselves with you, take additional consideration in recalling their name, and afterward, use it during the discussion. The way that you've recollected their name will win you regard and esteem.

Watch Your Stance

Alpha guys are bosses of their stance. Posing oneself as prohibitive, saved, or meek is known as a "low-power present." It will cause you to feel less sure, and you'll be seen as inaccessible and cold.

Changing your actual stance will change your brain processes. Standing tall, being open, and far-reaching is known as a "powerful posture." This makes your mind discharge dopamine, causing you to feel good and more sure. Studies by clinician Amy Cuddy indicated that individuals who took a robust posture for two minutes before a meeting performed far superior to those who didn't.

Attempt this at present—it's known as the "Superman posture." Stand tall, widen your shoulders and chest, place your hands on your hips, and your feet shoulder-width separated—as though you're relentless and going to save the world. Hold this posture for 2 minutes, and you'll make your cerebrum discharge dopamine, and you'll feel more confident. The appeal comes from certainty.

Tune in and Pose Inquiries

Alpha guys likewise tune in. The old Greeks had an adage, "You ought to listen twice as much as you talk since you have two ears and one mouth." People appreciate sharing their biographies; giving somebody a stage to do this by posing inquiries and tuning in, rather than overwhelming the floor, will make you the sort of individual others need to be near.

Recall what Dale Carnegie stated, "Converse with somebody about themselves, and they'll tune in for quite a long time." But be real. Individuals will smell you being fake well in advance.

Cut Out Fillers and Expressed Stops

Alpha guys are clear communicators. Expressed delays ("ahh," "umm") and fillers ("like," "you know") will seriously squeeze your correspondence. Magnetic individuals are persuasive and articulate, and that comes from resolving their talking abilities.

Pay attention to your discussions and note how regularly you use fillers and expressed delays. Request that your companions call you out at whatever point you do. They're frequently utilized when you're uncertain of what to state. Try not to fear quiet, allow yourself to think, and pick the correct words to state. You'll clean up your discourse, and you'll be a more appealing speaker.

Reflecting - Step-by-Step Instructions to Be Enchanting

Alpha guys read non-verbal communication. People refer to something intriguing called "reflecting neurons," which usually permits you to copy others' body developments. We're social animals wired for network and connections—reflecting neurons enable you to interact with your environment. It's regularly oblivious—think about the last time you just folded your arms simultaneously, the other individual did.

Unpretentiously, reflecting the position and non-verbal communication of whoever you're bantering with will make them more agreeable and increment affinity.

Praises

Alpha guys cause others to feel incredible. Praises have been appeared to support individuals' confidence by up to 34 %. Individuals may not recollect precisely what you did or what you stated; however, they will consistently recall how you affected them. Magnetic individuals use praises and are deliberate about causing others to feel critical.

Whenever you're having a discussion, distinguish one thing that you could offer a decent remark about. Or then again, send an irregular email, card, or instant message telling a companion you like them, or energize them about something they've done as of late.

Start and Present Yourself

Alpha guys venture out. It's unexpected to see the vast majority remaining back and being reluctant in social and professional situations. Alluring individuals step up and present themselves and sparkle a discussion. It shows certainty through being dynamic as opposed to aloof.

Put aside any dread of judgment and any hesitance. Visually connect and make sure to recognize everyone if you go into a gathering discussion.

Recount Stories - The Most Effective Method to Be Beguiling

Alpha guys have dominated the specialty of recounting incredible stories, and it doesn't take long for individuals to begin gathering around them. Everybody cherishes a decent story. An individual's creative mind flashes up when they tune in to stories, and they feel as though they're living it.

One of the critical components and establishments of narrating is to 'open and close the interesting hole.' Raise a theme that will liven the interest of others. Talk with enthusiasm, use symbolism and feelings.

Watch Your Grin

Alpha guys grin in some cases. There are clashing examinations on the impacts of grins. In an examination by the University of British Columbia, 1,000 grown-up members evaluated the sexual allure of many pictures of the other gender. The scientists found that ladies were least pulled in to grinning and cheerful men.

Be that as it may, cocreator of the examination Alec Beall rushed and said, "This investigation investigated initial introductions of sexual fascination in pictures of the other gender. We were not inquiring as to whether they suspected these objectives would make a decent sweetheart or spouse—we needed their gut responses on lustful, sexual fascination."

A significant imperfection of the investigation is that it's missing context; individuals were just taking a gander at photographs. Furthermore, that is never the situation with social interactions— individuals care about how you introduce themselves—looking harsh and aloof all the time won't be seen well. Ladies are profoundly appealing to a comical inclination.

The key is to be vital to grinning. Different examinations have indicated that grinning sets off the mind's prize instrument similar to eating chocolate. Investigators have discovered that individuals whose smiles' identities are seen as reliable are easy to interact with, and obviously, this will add to your mystique.

Try not to be one-dimensional, but grin sometimes to be warm, to be unemotional on different occasions, and to pass on secrets.

Chapter 5: Manage Social Situations

Being an alpha male is a straightforward concept. Many men are too preoccupied with their hairstyles in modern times, keeping clean nails or the most Adonis-like body obtainable. Now I'm not saying these aren't all attractive traits in a man and aren't what make YOU attractive. They simply carry themselves however they want, without second-guessing. This is what makes you attractive. Now you have to DECIDE to become an alpha male or not—it's a choice, and everyone can become one. At first, it will be difficult and awkward, but it's a habit that has to be learned.

Now let's get into the specifics. It's the small differences that will separate the alpha male from normal men. Often, we will not pinpoint what exactly makes a man so damn attractive (neither will women). "They have it," all we end up saying is, "Wow! He looks great!" It is all about their body language and behavior. Some are born this way, and others learn to find it within themselves. Every man can become successful with women and garner more respect from their peers by making simple adjustments to their body language and behavior.

Let's now describe what an alpha male is. Some answers thrown around will be "the most seductive," others will say "the most confident," a leader who will loudly display his dominance or a prevalent answer, "the best-looking one." Although it is true, it is not the whole picture. You do NOT need to be handsome or extremely good-looking to be an Alpha Male. Many good-looking guys don't have "it." Always falling into the friend zone or other males do not take them seriously. On the other side of the spectrum, you will find men who are not good-looking at all, yet much more successful than their handsome counterparts. Why is this? Because being an alpha male is a mindset.

Females find alpha males attractive, and why is this? Women have a sixth unique sense that they have developed over millions of years of evolution. It gives them the ability to understand body language and find a valuable partner. It's all in the way you carry yourself, and this will send signals to everyone around you that you are the leader, the strongest man, and significantly the most valuable in the group. Luckily enough, an alpha male lives inside us all, and the ladies will melt when you bring him out to the surface. Remember, everything is sub communicated through body language. Many studies, the most popular one being from American psychologist Ray Birdwhistell state that in conversation, "Only 1/3 of all information comes from words while 2/3 come from subtle body language." Your mannerisms speak very loudly, friend, and we can all hear them loud and clear.

Step-by-Step Instructions to Stand Like an Alpha Male

Remain before a mirror sufficiently huge to see your whole body and ask yourself, "Do I look like an alpha male?" Try and check, whether just by you practically standing, if you are communicating your manliness or if you are showing certainty. If it is not the case, there are not many tips to take care of you at that point.

Stand Up Straight and Bring Your Chest Out: This is giving off the message that you are not afraid to attack or to be attacked.

Display Your Sexuality: Done by having your legs a little wider than shoulder-width. It will help give you a reliable and masculine look.

Straighten Your Neck: Keeping your head up and looking straight will give you a little more height and show others you are not afraid of confrontation. NEVER look away from people, at your feet or theirs.

Exercise: It will give you a better posture as well as a more exhaustive figure. You will also feel great and full of energy that will aid your overall Alpha Male aura.

Instructions to Walk Like An Alpha Male

Whether in the workplace, in the city, or in your number one bar, your walk will say a ton regarding yourself and be considered an initial introduction to many. Here's some exhortation to help make your walk as alpha male as could be expected under the circumstances.

Saunter: This will show that you are not afraid when you enter a room. Simply relax and take time with every step you take.

Shoulder Length Steps: Steps that are too short will make you look feminine or like a follower. On the other hand, too wide steps will make you look clumsy and not in control. Shoulder length steps are the ideal distance your feet should be traveling.

Smile: Smiles are contagious. Seeing a happy man walking down the street smiling will spread this feeling everywhere he goes.

The Most Effective Method to Sit Like an Alpha Male

Men will invest a fair measure of energy plunking down (I am presently situated while composing this), and you can wager that even sit, an alpha male can be seen far in advance. Here's how they do it.

Sit Straight and Comfortably: Take up as much space as you think you will need. Look relaxed and remember that the one reason why we sit is that we're tired of standing.

Show Your Torso: Lean back and show off your chest. Make sure you feel comfortable, and it will show that you are not afraid of confrontation.

Do Not Close Yourself Off: This includes crossing your arms across your chest or bringing out knees up to your torso (similar to curling up into a ball) because it will make you seem defensive.

The Most Effective Method to Look at People Like an Alpha Male

We've all heard the platitude that the eyes are our windows to our spirits. Along these lines, show individuals your spirit while investigating theirs. The intensity of your look is an excellent device. This is the way you do it.

Look Directly into People's Eyes

It's quite intense looking someone in the eye, and it shows that you are very engaged with each other even if you hold the stare for only a second longer than usual. Look at everyone when you enter a room and when you have a one-on-one conversation with someone (women mostly), alternate from one eye to the other, and then look at their mouth. It will put the image of you kissing her in her mind.

Step-by-Step Instructions to Behave Around Women Like an Alpha Male

How Alpha Males act around ladies is genuinely unique, yet when all is said in done, there are a couple of consistent attributes that each alpha male will share. I could compose an entire journal on this theme alone; however, here are the significant hints:

Do Not Care What Others Think About You: An alpha male has high self-esteem. He will behave well; however, he does it without fazed by the opinions of others. He will express his opinions, beliefs, and desires as honestly as possible. A beautiful woman intimidates beta males, but an alpha male will never feel overwhelmed or believe that he cannot be with that woman because he is not good enough. He wants her but does not need her.

Never Cross the Line: It varies from culture to culture. In general, playing touching and hugs is fine, but grabbing her ass anywhere apart from within the bedroom is way over the line and unacceptable.

Be A Little Naughty and Playful: In other words, flirt. An alpha male will enjoy the company of beautiful women and will

39

let his inner true-self free. This means sitting next to a girl, talking about the weather when you honestly want to say she looks beautiful and impressive in her sexy dress is NOT being honest, and women will pick up on this.

Become Well-Mannered and Be a Gentleman: Women love a man with good manners and a great head on his shoulders. Watch some of the top 100 movies of all times and see which ones you like and do not like, then develop a small opinion of them. Read the top 100 books ever written because there is a reason so many people read them, so find out why and develop an opinion on them as well. Women LOVE a man who knows what he enjoys and does not enjoy, but even more, a man who knows why.

Talk to a Lot of Women: This is not as much of a trait but a practice. By talking to so many different types of women (women you find beautiful, young, old, attractive, dull, etc..), you will become comfortable around them and realize that women are just like any other human being out there. Just keep in mind that you are a confident alpha male. Show them all that you feel great in your skin.

Chapter 6: Improve Communication

The Medium Is the Message

I disdain the term "blended signals" or "blended messages." Usually, there's not much being imparted, and instead, it's a disappointment (headstrong or not) to peruse what a lady is conveying to a man. The average person tends to 'get' precisely what a lady has inferred with her words. However, it takes practice to peruse her conduct and even more practice to apply that understanding.

At the point when a lady goes from hot to cold and back again; the message is that she regrets something; you're not her primary goal; she's pondering among you and what she sees is a superior possibility, you were better-looking when she was smashed, and so forth—the message ISN'T the 'uncertainties,' the message IS her dithering and how her conduct shows it.

Ladies with a high-interest level (IL) won't confound you.

At the point when a lady needs to screw you, she'll figure out how to screw you. On the off chance that she's fluctuating between staying with you from that point, or rather settle for some time to taste other different plates. On the off chance that she figures it out for herself and seeks after you, at that point, you are still playing in her game, and you keep up the estimation of your thoughtfulness regarding her. It's the point at which you calmly take your time thinking about what enchantment equation will bring her around.

Most folks believe that "blended messages" or befuddling conduct from a lady is basically because of her failure (for reasons unknown) to make an exact translation of why she's acting in such a way. Typically, this ends up with a person getting so stuck with a solitary, single young lady that he would prefer to make concessions about her behavior that perceiving the truth about it. It's far simpler to call it "blended messages" or count on the old chestnut of how flighty and irregular ladies are when the truth is told, and it's essentially reasoning to keep themselves on the snare, as it were, because they do not have any genuine and suitable alternatives with different ladies in their lives.

A lady that has a high IL in a person has no need—and less inspiration—to participate in practices that would, in any way, compromise her status with him. However, a test is all the more effectively unmistakable when you consider the setting where they're conveyed.

As a rule, ladies tell the total truth with their activities, and they impart it in a manner that men can't or won't comprehend. As a behaviorist, I'm a firm devotee to the idea that the best way to find veritable inspiration or potential purpose is to notice a person's conduct. All one requires to do is think about conduct and its consequences to associate the intention behind it. A lady will communicate a considerable amount of data and certainties to a man if he's ready to acknowledge her conduct, not solely her words, as the measure for what she is really like. Likewise, he should comprehend that the reality she sells out in her conduct is frequently not what he needs to acknowledge.

We get disappointed because ladies impart uniquely in contrast to what we do. Ladies communicate secretly, and men communicate unmistakably. Men pass on data; ladies pass on inclination. In relating data, men organize content while ladies organize context.

One of the great confusions encouraged by feminization in the last 25 years is this assumption that ladies are just as normal and slanted to insightful critical thinking like men. This is the consequence of an equalizing mindset that deceives men into accepting that ladies don't behave and think in a unique form in contrast to men. That is not to limit ladies as capable issue solvers in their own right, yet it flies in the face how ladies set about an explicitly female type of communication.

Many many examinations outlining the regular limit ladies have for extraordinarily complex types of communication—to the point of demonstrating their neural pathways are wired suddenly—are signals gladly waved by a feminized media as confirmation of ladies' intrinsic benefits. Yet, as men, we're required to acknowledge that she 'signifies what she says, and she says what she implies.' While more than a couple of ladies like to draw upon this as identification of some sort of predominance, it doesn't imply that what they convey is more significant or how they impart it is more effective—simply that they have a more prominent ability to comprehend subtleties of communication than men do.

The most straightforward representation of this generational sex switch is to notice the specialized techniques for the "strong" ladies that the media depict as infamous fiction today. How would we know if she is a resilient lady? The main sign is that she communicates in a prominent, data-focused, manly way—she communicates like a man.

You don't have to be mystic to comprehend ladies' hidden messages, but you should be perceptive. This frequently requires a persistence that most men don't have, as they consider ladies as deceptive, whimsical, or scheming if the name fits. Indeed, even to the adequately wise men—and take the required mental notes to observe it going on around them—it appears to be wasteful and nonsensical.

Furthermore, is there any good reason why it wouldn't? We're Men. We convey our messages, by and large, exactly as we speak them, tackling the issue gruffly and forthrightly, and then proceeding onward to the following. Ladylike communication appears to be crazy; it is a profoundly useless type of communication—to be more explicit, it's a whimsical type of communication. It is just like children! They state a particular something and do another.

Indeed, they do. Furthermore, as a rule, they get what they're genuinely after—consideration. Ladies are insane. However, it's a determined insanity. Hidden messages baffle us just as much as apparent communication disappoints ladies. Our language has no quality for them—that is why we appear to be imbecilic or basic, best-case scenario, to ladies. We settle for data as our groundwork—not the hidden subtleties that make communication charming for ladies.

This is a similar explanation we consider female communication as being jumbling, confounding, and arbitrary, in any event, when it appears that they are making sincere endeavors to convey their ideas. The thing that matters is that our disarray and dissatisfaction are put to their definitive use. Since ladies stay

45

mysterious, arbitrary, unreasonable animals that men can't help wanting to change, yet can generally pardon; they can work unhindered towards their objectives.

As men, we'll state, "Insidious, indecent and manipulative lady! Shape up and make the best choice, saying one thing at that point doing another makes you a faker!" And this is our judicious nature unmistakably making itself understood in uncovering a lady's hidden messages, as an appeal to ethical quality, but it doesn't work. This is because ladies instinctually realize that their sexuality is their first and best office, and using hidden messages is the best strategy.

Advances to ethical quality work in support of herself since all she requires do concur with a man's apparent appraisal of her, and unexpectedly, he believes he's 'breaking through to her.' As men, we have got so adapted by the "feminine mystique" to anticipate that a lady should be tricky with us that when she abruptly inclines toward manly communication structures and turns to our own, clear specialized strategy and concurs with us, it appears to be she's had a revelation or a mental breakthrough, and we think, "Goodness, this one's truly exceptional, 'high caliber,' and appears to get it." That is since it suits her conditions to do as such—at the point when it doesn't, the feminine mystique is there to clarify it all away.

Have you ever been in a social setting, possibly a gathering or something, with a sweetheart or even a lady you might be dating and, out of nowhere, she says to you secretly, "Ooh, did you see the messy look that bitch just gave me?!"

You were in that general area in her actual presence, saw the young lady she was referring to, yet didn't enroll a thing. Ladies' hidden type of communication is conspicuous as that of a five-year girl. Ladies like to battle in the mental, while young men battle in the physical.

In a gathering, young ladies battle for predominance with the danger of segregation from the gathering. "I won't be your friend any longer if..." is the same amount of a danger to a girl as, "I'm going to punch you in the face," is to a boy. This dynamic becomes substantially more mind-boggling as young ladies enter pubescence, immaturity, and adulthood; yet they utilize a similar mental method of battle.

Their secretive method of communication through insinuation, non-verbal communication, appearance, sub-correspondences, motions, and so forth passes on unquestionably more data than our obvious, all on the table, method of conveying does. It might appear to be more useful to us as men, yet our strategy doesn't fulfill a similar reason.

47

Ladies appreciate the emotional connection more than the data being transmitted. It is not just another issue to be addressed, the emotional connection is essential. When a blockhead supplies her with all the information at one, the suspense is gone and he's not at test any longer. For what reason would she be intrigued? This is valid. However, the explanation that interest is gone is that there's no more potential for invigorating that need for communicating of her creative mind.

Finally, I should add that ladies do not use apparent communication when it fits their needs. At the point when a lady comes out and says something in a manner to leave no edge for confusion, you can wager she's been pushed to that point out of dread or sheer irritation when her undercover techniques don't work.

Similarly, men can and do dominate the specialty of hidden messages too. Extraordinary lawmakers, military pioneers, financial specialists, sales reps, and ace PUAs use all types of hidden messages to accomplish their objectives. It's wrong to consider hidden messages untrustworthy or irreverent, even in an ethical setting. It's an unfortunate obligation, similarly to individuals it is a necessary chore, and that means that whether chosen by men or ladies, it is not wrong unless you are doing it to deceive others.

Chapter 7: Hypnosis Techniques and How to Use Them to Rewire Your Subconscious

What Is Hypnosis?

Hypnosis is a psychological technique that involves the induction of a state of consciousness in which the individual loses the power of voluntary action. When a person is in a hypnotic state, they lose touch with the physical world and only focus or operate in a new world. In hypnosis, a new world/environment is created in the mind of the individual through visualization. A person can be heard talking to other people in the other world. When a person is in a hypnotic state, they are highly responsive to suggestions or directions. Hypnosis is used in therapy to help people who suffer from various ailments recover.

Although hypnosis is a practice that has been around for quite some time, it is still among the very controversial therapeutic techniques. While some psychologists suggest that a hypnotic state has no control over their actions, others argue that they cannot wholly lose their free will.

Generally, hypnosis can happen naturally or can be induced. Natural hypnosis happens without the person knowing or asking for it. Psychologists believe that an adult human being must go through a hypnotic state at least once per day. We will be looking at some examples of the hypnotic states later on. With that said, a hypnotic state that occurs naturally cannot be used to control your mind and actions. The hypnotic state that is induced works well when it comes to controlling your mind.

One of the ways of getting a person into a hypnotic state is by using music. If you play music with a tempo or rhythm of 45 to 72 beats per minute, you will probably transport a person's mind into a hypnotic state. The message within such music can be used to transform the thinking processes and a person's ideas. This is because the music plays at the same rhythm as your heartbeat. As a result, every beat of the song is perfectly synchronized with your mind.

The other option for induced hypnosis includes guided hypnosis. Guided hypnosis is the most common type of hypnosis, which takes place at a therapist's table. Hypnotists take the person through a visual journey that can transform the way of thinking of that person.

The Process of Hypnosis

The first step required for the process to be useful is to find a peaceful and calm place. Hypnosis has a greater chance of success in locations where there are minimal distractions from the environment. This enables the person to be hypnotized to concentrate and better picture the hypnotist's suggestions to him.

Of great importance is that the selected location must be where the patient feels secure. One will never be hypnotized if they are in a place where they feel that their security is at risk. For this step, given these conditions, an ideal place may be the home of the person to be hypnotized, as this is likely to be the place he would feel most calm and secure.

The next step is the preparation phase. Here, both parties will discuss issues surrounding the process and the desired outcome. Hypnosis is somewhat a guided creative process, and the hypnotist has to know what the patient wishes to get out of the process.

In our case, the patient will tell the hypnotist that he wishes to be relieved of the intense headache he feels. This exchange of information is crucial, as it will form the basis of the hypnotist's suggestions. It may be compared to a medical examination where the doctor endeavors to find out the problem ailing the patient. It is clear from this analogy that the success of the whole process is pegged upon this stage.

The hypnotist then gives the patient some instructions regarding the process, some of the things to expect, how to react to them, and what to do to relax and get into the zone. This is important, so that nothing comes as a surprise to the patient, thereby enabling the process to go on smoothly. Having prepared well, it is now time for the process to begin.

The hypnotist's first task is to get the patient into a relaxed state. This is done by giving a series of instructions to the patient. This stage of hypnosis is referred to as "the induction state of hypnosis."

The patient is expected to imagine these suggestions vividly. An example of a suggestion at this point may be, "Imagine that you are in a place that you like, a place that smells very good, surrounded by nothing but nature." The patient should respond to this suggestion by trying their best to picture themselves in the said place. In addition to these suggestions, the patient is often encouraged to control their breathing patterns during the induction phase.

This is an elaborate trick to shift the patient's focus from the conscious mind to the subconscious, which is tapped into during hypnosis. The more that this goes on, the more the patient sinks into a trance with anticipated cooperation from both parties.

The patient slowly forgets or completely disregards the immediate surroundings as the hypnotist guides them into a new reality.

Of course, the hypnotist will tell the trance's progress, gradually approaching the zone through suggestive guidance. To know the patient's stage, the hypnotist may suggest something that should make the patient happy; for example, "You are with your loved ones having a good time," then watch out for signs of internalization of this suggestion, such as a smile. Different moods can be suggested, and the corresponding physical signs assessed.

Once the hypnotist is satisfied that the patient is entirely receptive, he moves on to the then stage, which is crucial. This is where the problem at hand is handled. The suggestions made at this stage are directed towards altering the patient's thought processes and/or behaviors. Using our example, the hypnotist will tell the patient, "Imagine life without pain." Given the receptive state that the patient is in, they will visualize this suggested state by shifting focus from the pain in their head to this new suggested state.

Depending on the trance level that the patient achieves during hypnosis, the results will manifest for a significant amount of time even after the hypnosis session is done.

How to Learn Hypnosis?

Identify Your Field

Just like the case with learning anything else, you need to be clear beforehand which type of hypnotism you wish to learn. For example, in medicine, any good student ought to know the specialty area they would like to pursue.

One may opt to go for pediatrics, general surgery, neurosurgery, cardiology, dentistry, ophthalmology, or any other medical field. This helps the student know the areas to focus on for the best results.

The same goes for hypnosis. You may wish to learn hypnosis to do tricks to impress at street corners or on stage to gain the ability to help others through hypnotherapy, or you may wish to learn it for self-help through self-hypnosis.

These are all different types of hypnosis that require different study approaches and skills. For instance, hypnotherapy requires a human connection. You have to be able to engage a patient professionally while eliciting trust. Street hypnosis requires theatrics and stage performance capabilities.

Self-hypnosis requires a focused mind and a strong will and resolve to succeed. In conjunction with your reasons for your interest in hypnotherapy, these qualifications should be enough to guide you in the right direction.

Learn the Different Types of Suggestions

Several materials are available from which you can learn the different types of suggestions. The internet may be one such wealthy source. As a beginner, however, it may be necessary to begin with direct suggestions before moving on to indirect suggestions. Direct suggestions are simple to understand due to their straightforward nature and are shared with stage hypnosis, where people are 'instructed' to do something.

To study and understand how the direct suggestions work, you need to research hypnosis basics and how hypnosis works. You have to know of some of the essential requirements for hypnosis to work. A good example is knowing the answer to the question, "Why is the relaxation of the body and mind necessary to be receptive to suggestions?

If your interest in hypnosis is for street performance, then there is no need to study the indirect suggestions. If you are interested in hypnotherapy, this part is especially for you, and you should pay keener attention.

Having studied direct suggestions, you can now move into the more complex world of indirect suggestions. You must know the reasons why hypnosis works. For instance, you have to know that these suggestions all tap into a person's unconscious mind. Understanding this will give you an idea of why induction statements are framed the way they are.

Utilize Available Records and Videos

You must also understand that people are unique, and as such, they require personalized induction statements and suggestions for the best results.

To understand how this is done, you will need to go through different records of hypnotherapy sessions and try to figure out why the suggestions you read were appropriate for that particular patient. You can download several records such as these from the internet and watch videos of recorded hypnotherapy sessions.

In addition to records and videos, several journals have been written on the subject. Utilize these and you will be on your way towards learning to be a good hypnotist.

Practice What You Learn

An essential part of any study is practice. Find willing volunteers and continuously try to put whatever you learn into practice. You may be surprised at the outcome after just a few practice sessions with willing volunteers.

Please take note that to hypnotize someone successfully, you first need to be able to captivate them.

This means that you need to be able to tell a riveting story to draw someone's attention before you begin issuing induction statements. This is something you can practice with your friends and family, even without their knowledge. You need to monitor their attention spans as you speak. This will help you know and master different attention triggers for different people.

Chapter 8: The Science and Psychology of Self-Discipline

Self-discipline is generally an act of will, so it is crucial to understand how the human mind works. This is done to convert understanding to a greater sense of self-control. Over millions of years, the human being has evolved into an even more complex brain. As a human endeavor, psychology has shed some light on the mysteries of the mind, finally allowing us to see how things affect or motivate people and how our environment affects how we react to things that occur.

Self-Image

The way a man perceives himself affects how he reacts to the world. This is shaped by how he was raised or the kind of people that have surrounded him. The environment he grew up in has shaped how he sees himself. Some men have low self-esteem, which makes them believe that they are unworthy of good things or incapable of achieving perfection.

On the other hand, others have an inflated sense of self-worth, and they believe that they deserve everything without actually having to do much. These men, though they may seem powerful on the outside, are hollow. Cracks on their tough shell will show overwhelming insecurity that they have spent a lifetime hiding. If a man is on the quest to become a true alpha male, he must know the truth about himself and not give in to insecurity or the temptation to take the easy road by merely hiding under a facade.

However, there can be no guarantee that we will be able to understand ourselves immediately; and in fact, even psychology has not been able to get us a definite answer. But if your goal is to become an alpha male, you must be open to feedback. Negative feedback serves as a way for the man to detour from the path he has taken and improve himself. Focusing on negative feedback, however, won't do much good.

Negative feedback only works as a way to know if we are going the right way. However, you must discern whether or not the feedback comes from trustworthy and reliable sources. Often, in the interest of politicking, people tend to lie about what they think of you. Thus, you must only accept feedback from the people you trust to be brutally honest, such as a mentor or even enemies. Enemies have no interest in you and, by definition, hate you to the core. So, they will have no interest in sugar-coating anything. They will be absolutely and brutally honest.

It is wise not to be too emotional about what they have to say, instead, take it as a way to improve and achieve—not for them, but yourself—the ideal you want to reach, or the movement you are fighting for.

Locus of Control

A man on the path to self-improvement must find out whether he blames others or himself for what happens to him. If the man blames others all the time for everything that happens to him, it can be said that his locus of control is external, which means that he lets go of his power to fate or "destiny." This is the weak man's approach, especially if he believes that he cannot change anything that happens to him. He is weak-minded and weak-willed, and he thinks that whatever happens to him is because of random events or other people—this is a lazy and weak approach to life.

On the other hand, a man whose locus of control is internal tends to see everything as his fault, and if this goes to the extreme, he ends up being too overwhelmed by what is happening to him and even to the world. He might blame himself for something that happened to someone unrelated to him—this is unrealistic. We go back to the topic of self-image: The alpha male must have the right information about himself to act upon it.

The alpha male must be balanced and have a notion locus of control, so he must take responsibility for what he does. Taking responsibility strengthens the ability to take more significant risks, and it allows him to step outside of his comfort zone.

Classical Conditioning

To challenge the idea that psychology was an armchair pseudoscience, the behaviorist movement, which included the psychologist Ivan Pavlov, brought the scientific method into the field through experimentation. Pavlov was able to show the process of training and conditioning by measuring how much dogs salivated every time a bell is rung to signify food. After the experimenter rings the bell, he puts the food out. Soon, even when he does not bring out food, the bell's mere ringing has been shown to make the dogs react as if to get ready for food. This is called conditioning, and another way to apply this concept is reward and punishment.

People and animals tend to stay from punishment, and they tend to look for rewards. So, rewards will make us keep doing what we were doing to get that reward's pleasure. Punishments work the other way around, so the balance of both reward and punishment will effectively condition a person to a certain kind of action. Because we were born with the capacity to rule ourselves, we can consciously apply it to ourselves to achieve the kind of action we want to learn. Ask yourself how much pain you will get if you don't take action. For example, how much pain will you get if you don't study for your exam? Maybe you will not graduate. Now think about the short term pain of studying versus the long term pain of not graduating. Now think of the reward or pleasure you will get if you do the study. You will graduate with a degree and be respected by others. So, in this way, you can trick yourself into doing things that you don't feel like doing.

Psychology of Motivation

When people are asked who will win between a lion and a man in an arena, most people answer the lion because it is more powerful, and it has evolved to be stronger than the man. Unless that man is the mythical Hercules, the lion will no doubt devour the man. However, this does not consider the evolution that humanity has gone through in the past millions of years. The human has evolved a more complex brain and the ability to innovate and create weapons. Thus, a fairer fight would be between a lion and a man armed with weapons?

Humans are more complex than animals, and the difference is evident in our desire to become more significant than ourselves. This book is already a testament to that. Thus, in motivating a man to become better than himself, he must know what he is fighting for. He needs a goal and a way to know whether or not he has achieved it. Not knowing what he is fighting for, even the hardened warrior will fail. A man with a purpose is unstoppable.

Once the man has decided on his goal, he must begin to act. Success is being and doing what you want now, and that can only be achieved if you act immediately and act as if that success is already present now. Soon, even without thinking about it, the goal will have already been reached. It is also essential to trust in the process or habit through the continuous application of self-discipline.

Chapter 9: Atomic Psychology

Guys with Good Bodies Get Good Results

In today's world, the physical is your gateway. If you look like a fat slob, people are going to think you're incapable. They'll stereotype you as some sort of sloth—a man that is too big for his own good. They'll see you like a heart attack waiting to happen. Companies may not want to take a risk on you. After all, why should they invest in you if you haven't invested in yourself?

Why should they risk it if you're in bad shape?

And even if you aren't morbidly obese, being a little bit unfit will hurt you. It will hurt your dating prospects, your job prospects, and generally hurt others' perceptions of you.

The problem is that many men don't do what they can to be the healthiest they can.

It doesn't matter what you look like. The vast majority of us don't look like a movie star, and we, as sure as hell, don't have the physique of a professional athlete. For these reasons, a lot of us feel like it doesn't matter. We accept that our genetics aren't ideal, but we throw in the towel.

But why? Why do so many beta males continue to make excuses for why they can't work out? Is it because they're afraid to be seen in a gym? Do they fear the pain of working out or the long-term commitment? Do they tell themselves that they're too tired after a day of work or that they don't have time?

Or are they just being plain lazy? The answer is all of the above.

See, beta males always have a 'reason' for why they can't work out. They get into a routine of neglecting their bodies; their minds feel crappy as a result they end up making their bodies fat, which makes their minds feel crappier—and the vicious cycle continues.

Because most guys struggle with getting started, they should start small. If you think you're out-of-shape and have a terrible body-image problem, take baby steps. First, find recreational sports leagues with others like you—who like a little bit of exercise while socializing. Purchase a pullup bar and some dumbbells. Start doing pushups and crunches, lift weights around your house, and go for runs where nobody can see your out-of-shape body slogging and sweating.

The point is to continue progressing. Nowadays, there are all kinds of gadgets and watches that can track your progress. Heck, feel free to share your metrics with Facejournal and Twitter if you want! Become an exercise nerd. What matters is that you chart your progress, see your improvements, and feel good about it.

Too many people are pessimistic about exercise. They don't seem to realize that exercise is a necessary part of healthy living. They don't seem to get that exercise will make them feel better. The human body is meant to move, not collect cobwebs.

But this doesn't mean you have to tear down your body with every workout. You don't have to redline every time you exercise. Merely getting your heart rate up consistently is good to start. After a while, it becomes significantly more comfortable.

When we exercise, our excuses disappear. Do you complain that you're too tired all the time to exercise? Well, guess what, sleepyhead... the more you exercise, the more endurance and energy your body and mind have.

People think that routine exercise will wear them out even more. This is false! Routine and moderate exercise will increase your vitality, improve your mood, and generally boost your physical and mental health. You'll also start to embrace other healthy things like eating.

And speaking of eating... If you don't eat well, you won't feel well. Not to mention you'll be carrying around some extra baggage that can't be good for you—unless your mission is to be a human cushion. So, eat well!

Yea, yea, yea, you've heard this one a million times before. Chances are you don't know where to start or—like exercising—lack the motivation. Well, here's a little motivation for you. You can eat well by eating clean foods. You can also eat clean foods and stay healthy. Oh, and you can eat clean and healthy, and do it cheaply.

So, what's your excuse now? Do we need to go into details about this one? I think not.

Lookup a million studies about how clean eating can enhance your performance, your well-being—the whole nine yards. You'll be surprised.

Listen, it's not hard. I know you probably think it requires some dramatic shift in your life, but it doesn't. More likely than not, you know your bad habits. You know if you drink too much soda, overeat ice cream or pack on too many beer calories. Eating clean is about eating in balance—some vegetables, fruits, dairy foods, and some meat. Don't try to eat anything by itself. Eat a combination every time you eat. Instead of snacking on Oreos, eat some bread with hummus or a banana. Instead of guzzling coffee, opt for green tea. Substitute fruit infusions for sugary beverages.

Just be smart. Choose the simple and healthy alternative and don't stress it. Think less about the things you're missing and focus on all the things you're getting. And if you find yourself craving those sugary sweets or delicious late-night meals, remind yourself of the truth. You're not missing anything. Seriously, you aren't. The only thing you're missing is processed chemicals, cancer-causing chemicals, and nutrient/vitamin-empty foods.

Does that sound like something you should be missing? You only have one body and one brain. Do you want to shovel shit into them like the cookie monster or turn them into a work of art?

Your choice.

Chapter 10: How to Manage a Relationship?

Do You Have the Right to Lead Her?

An old buddy of mine once disclosed a tale about how he was dismissed by an alluring young lady he was keen on. The intriguing part was that she was crying and being hurt by somebody, yet when he endeavored to reassure her, her response to him was calm, mean, and honestly... annoying.

At the point when he disclosed this story to me, I wanted to ponder about the suggestions. Naturally, he went into significantly more detail than I just did, as I had the option to break down the circumstance from top to bottom with him. Furthermore, after a couple of seconds of addressing and pontification, we showed up at an exceptionally straightforward motivation behind why his contribution of solace was the ultimate mood killer for her. It's basic: He didn't have the right to comfort her.

Before you can lead a lady, she must have a type of trust in you. My friend, however, his goals were right; even though he would have utilized her adversity to show his affinity to her, he was not the sort of man she could trust, at any rate, at least then. He was feeble, inadequate, and undoubtedly, a naturally disappointed sucker, and she knew it. Indeed, even in her undermined position, she would not permit herself to be helped by a man who came up short on the strength she longed for; she would rather feel no right (power) to comfort herself in her period of scarcity.

Facing a troublesome lady requires being legitimate. If she's giving you the business, you should have the option to attest your limits usually. A couple of events won't trick a lady into touch and involvement with managing men.

Even after you start confronting her, she will test you, again and again, to guarantee that the one time you guarded your limits was anything but a unique case. She needs consistency from you; the kind of consistency that can just come from a man who has not just figured out how to practice his clout in a relationship but, on the other hand, he's found out how to be an emphatic man.

Being confident with yourself implies that your attitude impacts your conduct. You're not dependent entirely on procedures. It almost means that your determination drives your nature and you can act without thinking too much. This is the thing that your lady will be searching for because, without steady shows of confidence on your part, she won't be persuaded by your 'once in a while' demonstrations of power.

70

As you've likely acknowledged at this point, what she needs is consistency from the man in her life. What's more, an ideal approach to guarantee that you're large and in charge usually is to move past the purpose of merely acting alpha and spotlight your energy on turning into a solid and confident man at your core—all things being equal.

Surrender Your Need for Coddling

On occasion, you don't know the meaning of 'pamper' is to treat in a liberal or overprotective manner. That implies, on the off chance, that you're a man who needs pampering, particularly from ladies, and at that point, with the end goal of having a sense of safety about yourself, you should be treated in a liberal or overprotective manner.

I was in middle school, and I was indeed having one of those days when things weren't turning out well. In biology class, I had this female educator that demanded giving the folks in our group trouble. She was another educator and thinking back; I understand that what she was doing was trying to see which folks she had supreme authority over the others and which of them would be bound to give her trouble.

On the day being referred to, she said something that was especially offending to me before the whole class. I felt hurt and

71

humiliated—and I looked like it. It was obvious that she had 'hurt my sentiments,' and she came over, put her arm around me, and apologized. Indeed, this occurred in middle school before EVERYONE. Trust me, I'm cringing as I write this.

So, for what reason do I raise this dull, agonizing, and unmanly memory that I pledged to keep a secret forever? Just for your advantage. In this little goody from quite a while ago, I required pampering. From that second on, she watched what she said to me, not out of regard, but out of pity. I got what I needed, which was to be disregarded. However, it wasn't because she regarded me.

My affectability shone through effectively, but different children in the class didn't have a similar sort of sympathy for me. I can disclose to you that much. I'm practically sure that that occasion caused a ton of middle school enduring that took me for a spell to address.

Thinking back, what I ought to have done was have a grown-up-like, 'cut-it-out" discussion with her at that point or react with arrogance and humor. Since she was so ready to "go there" with me, I ought to have had the guts to do likewise with her. Tragically, I didn't, and it will perpetually be an exercise of how not to react to undesirable quips or a lady's tests.

The Right Attitude

In regard to finishing a lady's assessments or sorting her out, it isn't what you say that matters the most, but by and large, it's the way you say it. At the point when a lady misbehaves with you or accomplishes something you believe is beneath her, you don't need to be discourteous, whiny, or furious to express your dismay or dissatisfaction. You don't need to be forceful; neither do you need to mope to communicate your assessments. Act like a grown-up male.

I genuinely feel that taking care of such circumstances should be finished with thoughtfulness, immovability, and a genuine worry for her prosperity.

Consider it along the lines of a dad. You love your youngsters, yet you need to do and make statements they won't care about because you have their eventual benefits on a fundamental level. You're not worried about how kids will perceive you during the hour of discipline. You're more worried about their prosperity, presently and later on. You decide to be seen as a 'miscreant' because that is the right thing at those moments. In particular, you're in every case reasonable and genuine with your decisions—regardless of how disagreeable they might be.

Men Who Care Too Much

Will you certainly remain in front of an audience and convey a discourse about something you trust in before a furious horde of thousands of ladies who energetically can't help contradicting all that you need to state? It's alright if you answered, "No." Well, not numerous men can.

Why? On the off chance that we take out the dread of public talking, it could just be because of the dread of having a disagreeable assessment. It could even be because of the dread of objection and dismissal—particularly by ladies. It very well may be because of the dread of being scrutinized and alienated by ladies. Or then again, it very well may be a direct result of these things together.

So, what's my point? Decent folks, weak, avoidant and timid men are prone to being "misconstrued" or disdained, particularly by ladies. They care a lot about people's opinions and spot their self-esteem under the group's control. What's more, for this situation, it's a horde of ladies.

It's terrible for a lady to be irritated with that kind of men, to consider them contrarily, or to feel utter scorn for them. Men like this will do pretty much anything to dodge angry circumstances with ladies just to forestall the extraordinary sensations of inconvenience that accompany it.

While it is significant for men to be aware of how they are seen by their honor (gathering of male companions, male tutors, and so on), it doesn't profit them—a similar way regarding the other gender. Getting not interested in whether a lady may consider you when you act dependent on your standards is quite possibly the most remarkable disposition shifts you can make as a man. The advantages of being an alpha man will amaze you and will be beneficial to how you experience a lady's tests. At the point when you're making an effort not to guess what she might be thinking to see whether she'll affirm what you need to state, you have a more prominent opportunity to act from a position of honesty.

Hyper-investigating what a lady may figure, say, do or feel, on the off chance that you follow that particular path, causes profound uneasiness. After some time, such tension transforms into dread. The sort of dread that makes you fix, haw, and second-guess each choice you need to make. It is anything but a beautiful picture to notice a man caught in a pen making as he surrenders his whole self to a lady.

How This Behavior Plays Out?

Such conduct happens in all the typical manners that accommodating people show. Now and then, it's inconspicuous, and on different occasions, it's not all that unpretentious, yet it generally shows itself in how a man communicates with a lady. Here's a short rundown of what these practices resemble:

- Selecting and editing your words, or tiptoeing with your style so as not to disappoint or stimulate a lady's displeasure in any way.

- Making provisional proposals to pick up her endorsement as opposed to clarifying explanations. For instance, "Nectar, I'm figuring we ought to eat Chinese food around evening time." This is a recommendation, and you're unmistakably sitting tight for her endorsement.

- Censoring your suppositions, conduct, and even your necessities to keep her glad and unwarranted.

- Thinking unreasonably about her opinions, or what she would say and do if you said what you would like to do.

- Trying to be unique to procure the endorsement of others.

If you do those things, then it is not difficult to concede that you have become a shell-of-a-man. Also, it's significantly harder to change what could be long stretches of detached, human satisfying propensities that may now characterize your relationships. You have to note that if live that way, you still have an opportunity for change and adjustment in your self-conviction, which can really renew your relationships.

Reclassify Your Self-Worth

A man's self-esteem ought not to be inseparably connected to the strength of his sentimental relationship. Envision how unpleasant it would be if the worth you put on yourself as a man is 100% subject to whether things are working out positively for you and your lady.

Chapter 11: Summary of the Key Points

In today's time, where masculinity is on the decline and there's a war being fought against masculine values, we must bring back the old values and stick to them. Society fears masculine values because; it doesn't understand them, which is why we're losing our strength. We're becoming more and more corruptible, by the way. We're becoming incredibly self-entitled and have started to rely too much on others. That is not how a real man behaves. We need to bring back real strength.

Be Self-Reliant

It's a quickly disappearing quality among men—and this trend is worrying. There's a growing sense of entitlement among people that makes us feel like we deserve the things we haven't earned yet. Don't accept a life of dependency. Sustain yourself and never look for a handout. This doesn't mean you can never ask for help; you can and should when you need it, but that shouldn't be your default way of thinking. Always repay the help you receive from someone.

Understand That Success and Happiness Require Hard Work

Never think that you were born into success. You always have to work for it and earn your success. Success and happiness in life don't come easy—whether you're talking about your professional life or personal life. You have to work for them.

Practice Self-Denial and Forget About Instant Gratification

We were born in a generation that is always seeking instant gratification. We have our credit cards, loans, and whatnot. It's become much more comfortable to buy things we don't need to impress people we don't even like. This attitude must change.

Forget Your Past and Don't Be Afraid to Dream of a Great Life

This one, despite being a tricky law, is significant. You have to do many trials and error before finding the right path for yourself, the thing you want to do, and the kind of man you want to become. It will help you if you do so.

Don't Be Afraid to Fight Even If You May Lose

Many of us are so used to living a comfortable life that the idea of a hard life scares us. But to rise above others, you have to defeat these fears. Don't fear living the life of an eternal warrior; it's the only way people will remember you. Teddy Roosevelt was a fighter, and so was Napoleon. But we shouldn't include only the ones who were fighters in the literal sense. Jobs was a fighter too, and so was Gandhi.

Accept Responsibility for Your Actions

The most significant and defining characteristic of a coward is that he never sees his fault. He always blames his failures on someone else. In this time, when honor is a fast-disappearing trait, it is the mark of a real man to own up to his mistakes. The vast majority of people no longer accept their mistakes. They always find an excuse or way to deflect the blame to someone else.

You cannot call yourself a man unless you are a man of honor.

Don't Be Afraid to Stand up to Your Principles and Values

A real man doesn't need numbers to support himself. He has the strength within himself to stand up to his values. Only the weak need numbers because they are cowardly and can't stand on their principles.

You shouldn't be attention-seeking. Our society is heading toward a future in which everyone is dependent on what others think of them—and it alters our thinking. We need to feel accepted, but taints our actions. If you want to be a true leader, walk to the beat of your tune and think for yourself. Be original and don't give in to the need to feel accepted by others.

Don't Be Afraid to Fail but of Never Trying

Do you know what a coward does? He never tries because he is afraid to fail. If you want to talk up the game, be sure you act on it. Don't make empty boasts among your friends and then step back. That's cowardly and something a real man should never do. Talk less and do more. An alpha male acts on his words and leaves a legacy for others to follow.

Practice Kindness But Not Weakness

"Give a man a fish, and you feed him for a day. Teach a man to fish, and you will feed him for a lifetime."

If you have a skill, teach it to others, because that's what people ultimately need. It's common for people these days to just throw money at their problems. But that's not a real solution. You should give your mind and your time to a problem—not just money.

Always be kind and help others, but be thoughtful too. Think about things, but act with due diligence. Being weak is not the same thing as being kind, so actually make an effort to know things. You should carry yourself, not want others to carry you. Every man wants to carry himself, and if you can find a way to give yourself that power. That is the greatest kindness you can ever show.

Never Turn a Blind Eye to Injustice

Men have protected their tribes and their people for thousands of years from beasts, nature and other men. Although that's not how the world works anymore, that doesn't mean you should give up so quickly these days. You should still be protective of people, especially those who are facing injustice. The world is a mean place filled with evil people who don't think twice before harming others. You should never turn a blind eye to this sort of injustice.

Never be afraid to stand against the majority. Even if there's an army in front of you and nothing but the wind behind your back, you must stand your ground against injustice. Don't cower in the face of danger.

Read as Much as You Can

Spend considerable time reading. Read about everything, including not just people who inspire you, but also those whose worldview differs from yours. It is the mark of a smart person to entertain an idea without accepting it or agreeing with it. If you happen to be a liberal, read something written by a conservative and deeply think about it—and vice versa. If you're a deeply religious person, read something written by an atheist. Read about science, economics, business, sports—everything. Learn about different cultures and politics. Reading is a gift, and you can learn more than you can imagine from it. So, get out of your comfort zone often and just read!

Be Just and Fair

Our idea of fairness is constantly being bastardized and diluted. This is because moral qualities are disappearing from society and a growing number of people want what they haven't earned yet. It's the mentality of the weak. Yes, some people need and deserve our help and it's on us to help them. But you should never envy what another man has. It's dangerous and unmanly to do so. Don't expect someone else to give you a part of what they have simply because you think you didn't have the same opportunities in life. That's a weakness.

Unplug Weekly

We become disconnected from our values and our mission when we get too lost in the noise of everyday life. Our beliefs and intentions become clouded and we lose sight of our purpose. Silence is golden as it can be your most valuable friend in life. We need it to reconnect with ourselves and to our purpose. It gives us clarity because it is in silence that we recharge. We rediscover ourselves and hear our doubts and fears.

Don't Live on the Internet

If you want to be a real man, don't live on the Internet. Ground yourself in the reality of the physical world, and don't get caught up in what people think of you on Facebook. Don't worry about the number of "likes" on your photos or how many "friends" you have. These things don't matter, because your real friends will stay in contact with you despite Facebook. Show the world who you are.

Be Chivalrous

Chivalry is dying and fast. There are many reasons, and one of which is that men no longer want to go the extra mile. They just don't care enough to do chivalrous deeds, and chivalry is not being taught to them anymore. But a real man needs to be polite. A good man lives by this code and always follows it.

Have a Grand Adventure at Least Once in Your Life

If you're planning to go on a long trip to a foreign land, here are some tips:

Have a Sound Credit Card: You might not realize it, but soon in a couple of years, hopefully, you will have enough points to cover most of your trips.

Don't Stay in a Hotel: You can't expect to shell out hundreds of dollars every day if you want to stay for an extended period. Instead, you should try something like Airbnb or Couchsurfing. It's much cheaper that way, and you can still earn some money while doing freelance work. You can easily make friends via Couchsurfing and stay with them, or if that doesn't seem good enough to you, you can use Airbnb to get the right places for as low as $500 a month. If you don't want to have a very lavish lifestyle on your trip, definitely check out Airbnb.

Don't Be Afraid: Do whatever you genuinely want to do and go anywhere without fear of getting lost or stranded. It will help you improve your survival skills and make you a stronger man.

Laugh Daily and Don't Take Yourself Too Seriously

Life is nothing without joy, and you need to loosen up at times to enjoy life. I know all of the real men, whether living or dead, know not to take themselves too seriously and laugh a lot. They have a good sense of humor, which everyone appreciates. They also don't mind laughing at themselves.

A man who can laugh at himself is as secure in himself as he can be.

Speak with Your Actions and Not Words

A real man talks less and does more. It's not your words that make you a big man; it's your actions. You should be the embodiment of toughness, humility, and pride. Vanity and envy shouldn't even come close to you. John Wayne wanted to portray a real man's qualities in all of his silver screen characters because he wanted to inspire the younger generation.

Be The Best at What You Do

To become your best, you have to attempt to be at your best at all times. Life isn't about merely existing; so, whatever you do, do it with all of your heart. Give it your 100%.

Chapter 12: Work until Finally Acquire Your Identity Change in 21 Days

So far, this book has provided all of the tools, insights, and directions you need to begin transforming your life into that of a true alpha male. However, one more piece of the puzzle needs to be put in place before the big picture can be realized. That piece is setting goals. The importance of setting goals simply cannot be overstated. While many believe that the reasons they are unable to turn their dreams into reality are a lack of resources, time, or energy, the simple truth is that most people fall short due to a lack of goals. Goals are what turn dreams into achievable tasks because actions can be taken daily to reach the desired destination. In short, goals are what turn abstract and intangible dreams into quantifiable reality. Therefore, to change your life in any way, shape, or form, you must begin by setting the necessary goals.

What Exactly Is a Goal?

Many people mistakenly associate dreams with goals. Therefore, if you want to be rich, you might say your goal is to be rich.

Unfortunately, this isn't entirely accurate. It would be more correct to say that your dream is to be rich. The goal is the step or set of steps in the plan that will lead you to that dream. Knowing the destination is just the first step; it is the step of knowing your dream.

The next step is deciding how you will get there. You probably need to plot your journey. You may have to stop once or twice depending on how far you have to go. How long it will take, which paths to choose, and whether you need to stop along the way are all part of planning the journey. This is the act of setting goals. Each path you enter is a goal, and each stop is a goal; every element of the journey—including when you leave and when you return—is a goal. They are measurable actions that will lead you to your dream.

This is where most people fall short. By mistaking the dream for a goal, they never take the time to plot the course to take themselves to where they want to be. They usually never even take the first step since they are unsure which step to take. When you have your course plotted, you know where to go and when to go, allowing you to take the actions needed to achieve your dream effectively.

Methods for Effective Goal Setting

As with anything else in life, simply setting goals isn't always enough. Instead, you need to set the right goals in the right way. This will make all the difference when it comes to achieving the goals you set. Fortunately, there is a simple formula for practical goal setting, known as the "SMARTER" goal system, and it works like this:

- **Specific:** Make sure always to set specific goals. Instead of saying you want to lose weight, set the goal of reaching a target weight, such as one hundred and eighty pounds. This is a specific goal in which you can easily track your progress.

- **Measurable:** The next step is to set a measurable goal. In reaching a target weight, you need to measure where that weight is from where you currently are. Thus, if you weigh two hundred pounds, then your measurable goal is to lose twenty pounds.

- **Actionable:** This is where you begin to plot your course concerning achieving your overall goal. If you want to lose twenty pounds, you can set actions such as eating healthier foods or exercising regularly. This turns the goal from an ambition into an achievable action.

- **Realistic:** Sometimes, people make the mistake of setting goals that are too big to achieve. In the case of losing twenty pounds, you might choose to break the goal down into four smaller goals of losing five pounds per week. This takes the stress out of an "all or nothing" scenario, giving you easier targets to reach.

- **Time-Bound:** This part of goal setting has two elements. The first element is when you start. If you want to lose weight, decide on when you will start taking action. The next element is the deadline. This is when you hope to achieve your goal. Thus, your goal should now be to lose five pounds in one week, starting tomorrow.

- **Evaluate:** When you have your measurable goal and your timeframe, you can begin evaluating your progress. If you have only lost one pound halfway through your seven-day deadline, then you can look at either increasing your efforts—perhaps by engaging in more exercise, eating better, or extending the deadline. In the end, it's always better to alter the goal than to give up on it altogether.

- **Reward:** The final phase of goal setting is to reward yourself for the progress you make. For example, each time you lose five pounds, you can choose to reward yourself by purchasing that DVD you have wanted for a while or some other relatively inexpensive item that acts as an incentive. Not only will this encourage you to keep going, but it will also program your mind to crave achieving the goals you set. When you achieve the big goal, you can go clothes shopping as a reward—treating yourself to a new wardrobe that will show off your new look.

Setting SMARTER goals increases your chances of achieving those goals, which will change your life in a couple of very significant ways. First, your self-confidence will grow stronger and stronger with every goal you achieve. Therefore, as you achieve more goals, you will grow in confidence, giving you the courage to chase more and larger goals. The second way that this will change your life is that it will increase your success overall. Each goal will improve your life in some way. Therefore, as you accomplish more goals, you will be eager to set even more goals, which will improve your life exponentially, and enable you to create the life of your dreams.

Specific Goals for the Alpha Male

Now that you know the importance of goals and setting them. The final step is to set specific goals for an alpha male. The following are some goals that will help you to develop the alpha male lifestyle you desire and deserve:

- **Improve Your Image:** This takes many forms, including the clothes you wear, your physique, and even your grooming habits. Therefore, you must break this overall goal down into smaller and more manageable goals. The first will be to improve your hairstyle. Give yourself thirty days to find a stylist who will help you achieve the right look for you. Then you will want to work on getting your weight to ideal. Give yourself thirty days to achieve a specific weight (if that is a goal that is achievable in this timeframe). Finally, you will want to improve your wardrobe. Give yourself another thirty days to change your clothing style, giving you the alpha male look that will attract all the right attention. Make this your last step, as you will want to be at your right weight and have a hairstyle ready to define which clothes work best for you.

- **Improve Your Self-Image:** This is another goal that will have many aspects. One aspect is establishing your values. Take a week or two to carefully contemplate those things that truly define who you are and the life you want to live. Once you have chosen your values, you need to integrate them into your day-to-day life in the form of your choices and the actions you perform. Then increase your positivity. Begin spending time around positive people, feeding off of their energy and using them as inspiration for chasing your dreams. Finally, take thirty days to work on developing your charm. The more charming you act, the more charming you will feel. This will increase your self-esteem as well as your self-confidence when interacting with other people.

- **Chase your Dreams:** Once you have improved yourself from the inside out, it is time to start turning your dreams into reality. Take some time to decide what you want to achieve. If it is winning the perfect woman, landing the perfect job, or achieving some other life-changing ambition, make that your purpose. Once you have chosen your purpose, start setting goals on how to reach that destination. Give yourself thirty days to come up with a destination and a solid plan to reach that destination. Use the SMARTER method to break your overall goal into smaller and more achievable goals that can be measured and tracked effectively. Now that you have developed the heart, mind, and appearance of a true alpha male, there is no dream beyond your reach. Now you can start creating the life you have always wanted, the life of your dreams.

Chapter 13: What Does a Woman Want from a Man?

The sort of lady that will make your life significantly more satisfying is the sort of lady that needs to be driven by a man who realizes how to manage struggle and settle on wise choices.

The better you become at making shared benefit arrangements when managing others and practicing dynamic control, the more powerful your dynamic will be. Savvy instinct and balance are two qualities that a decent leader should have.

Building up your own relational and administrative skills is essential for relating with the other gender because of the straightforward reality that ladies are organically intended to search out a leader to offer themselves to both genuinely and inwardly.

Consider everything in nature because the things in animals also apply to human beings.

In the set of all animals, the alpha male will pick the best of the bundle. He chooses what region he needs and which females he needs to mate with. Nature has planned a framework whereby the best guys will reproduce and virtually manage everything. The alpha male is the person who assumes responsibility for a gathering, passes on his qualities, and leads and ensures the gathering that he's assumed responsibility for.

Genuinely, just the strongest ones endure.

Even though things aren't as fundamental in the human world, it's still basically dependent on a similar reason.

Men who are in the spotlight are profoundly compelling to women and exceptionally regarded by them. Those men can do things that others can't do; they can have whoever ladies they want.

Although most men turn out badly, some men center around the outward indications of male strength and consider to go the solitary way to pull in and keep a top-notch lady in their life. They feel that crazy and great looks, distinction, or fortune are their pass to getting and keeping the lady they had always wanted.

They've been lied to.

The outward indications of accomplishment and force all speak of something different. Any man who is happy and sufficient enough can be the best version of himself.

Things like abundance, force, distinction, and other attractive qualities, just speak to the initiative in some structure or another. It outlines a person who stands apart from the group, somebody to appreciate, regard, and follow.

Fortunately, those of us who may not be incredibly attractive, rich or notable do have a battling chance at pulling in and keeping a lady that is perfect, savvy, faithful, and cherishing.

By creating authority characteristics, you will find that ladies become all the more customarily attracted to you; however, you'll also start to draw in more accomplishment into your life.

The Most Effective Method to Remain Calm in Conflict

Figuring out how to adequately deal with struggle is fundamental if a decent lady is genuinely going to put her trust in you as a competent leader. Much the same as building muscles, you'll develop enthusiastic fortitude and strength the more you practice your dynamic capacity all through the clash.

Furthermore, much like the more loads you use, the more muscle you can assemble, and the more serious the contention, the more energetic balance you can create.

Whenever you're confronted with a troublesome circumstance, figure out how to remain outside of it and 'respite.' Rather than responding to your current circumstance, pick a reaction.

This is the place where your excellent mindset becomes possibly an essential factor. Make an incredible certification or some other type of positive self-talk that will make you mindful of how you act and react in a troublesome circumstance.

Your expression MUST match your current state and fill you with feelings when you state or consider it. For instance, something like:

"I am cool, quiet, sure, and in charge. Nothing or nobody can make me lose my self-control. I am a confident person, and I settle on the best choices consistently. At the point when everybody around me is losing control, I am getting cooler and more settled. I am the go-to fellow when things turn crazy. I AM THE MAN, and everyone knows it."

This is an excellent reason for a fantastic attestation or self-talk of your own, yet recollect that it should fill you with feeling the more you rehash it to yourself.

I can promise you that if you build up the propensity for rehashing a bunch of affirmations to yourself in private and in any event when a contention emerges, you WILL start to see positive outcomes.

I need to recommend a book that I'd encourage you to peruse at any rate twice. It's called, "What to Say When You Talk to Yourself," and it was composed by the top-rated creator, Dr. Shad Helmstetter. The title of the journal essentially says it all indeed. However, he broadly expounds on the most proficient method to change your life by changing the discussions you have with yourself.

In a real sense, your self-talk directs your speculation, which manages your activities, and thus gives you the outcomes in your day-to-day life. All in all, when you change your self-talk, you'll transform yourself.

On the off chance that the arrangement of expressions I proposed before appear to be altogether too long to your state when you get into a type of contention or unpleasant circumstance, simply utilize a more limited form:

"I am in charge of my feelings. I am fearless and confident. I settle on magnificent choices. I am a daring man with monstrous balance and force."

Try using self-talk in both private and public settings to the point when it becomes your mantra. Get passionate about it and imagine yourself as an unflinching mountain encompassed by a noisy storm.

Honestly, pictures encourage a great deal to pass on the message of intensity and balance to your psyche.

Practice and see what works for you, but don't neglect it as some psychobabble fix that won't get you results. Trust me, the psyche is more impressive than what the vast majority of us understand. Since your craving is to turn into the ideal person for the lady you had always wanted, you'll need to do your best to the most extreme to get the outcomes you truly need.

Figuring Out How to Make Better Decisions

The one who assumes responsibility and shows activity in doing things is an appealing catch to a great lady. Yet, how would you become the sort of man who uses sound judgment reliably? There are two different ways that come to my mind as write that have worked for me. Here they are:

First, study the lives of different pioneers and extraordinary men who live or have carried on with prosperous and fruitful lives so you can realize what decisions they made for the duration of their lives. Read books that can help you improve your confidence and aptitudes, as turning into a pioneer requires breathtaking dynamic abilities.

As I've said before that the memoirs of great men, just as the books are written by them, are loaded up with knowledge and shrewdness for those of us needing to turn out to be better leaders.

Finding out about such people will help outfit your psyche with bunches of instances of what decisions these men made when confronted with affliction and impossible conditions.

Not only will the perusing of books on and by extraordinary men assist you with settling on better choices, but you'll be building up a propensity that will make you undeniably more effective throughout everyday life and unmistakably more appealing to a great lady. Your reasoning will be so remarkable and unique— concerning most of the folks around you—that she won't have the option to oppose looking into you.

The following method to improve your ability to use sound judgment is to start settling on MORE choices... significantly more. Step up to the plate whenever the open door emerges by putting forth a conscious attempt to present and execute an answer for an issue. Try not to stay shy and quiet because you trust that others will 'assume responsibility' on the off chance that you have a recommendation or a definite inclination. Be the one to 'settle on the decision' or possibly be the one to propose a "game-plan."

Likewise, be sure that as you increment the number of choices you make, you additionally make choices that are somewhat riskier. Start settling on extreme choices, and make them while being aware of how you are at that exact second settling on an intense choice. Use the immediate methodology and decline to tiptoe around an issue.

At the point when you become mindful of the measure of choices that you make on an everyday premise, you put yourself in a condition of creative force. This means you'll start to understand that you are answerable for your outcomes throughout everyday life.

You are liable for your future. You are the expert of your destiny and the commander of your spirit.

As you settle on a tremendous amount of these choices every day, make them unflinchingly. If you choose a game-plan and it doesn't work out, don't stress yourself over it.

Simply advise yourself that you'll settle on a vastly improved choice whenever around—this is the place where utilizing great positive self-talk will prove to be useful.

Settle on the drastic decision and make it intentionally. A few choices you'll need to make won't assist you with winning any ubiquity challenges. However, the objective isn't to be enjoyed but to have uprightness with yourself and direct your course.

Take Care of Business

A great lady adores a man who can be relied on to settle on extreme choices.

Why? Because it shows her that you're confident, self-coordinated, and ready to focus on things. Besides, she needs a man in her life to settle on those intense choices that she likely wouldn't have any desire to make.

Be That Man

At the point when a man understands what bearing he's living by, he turns out to be substantially more alluring to the other gender. When he realizes where he's going in life, he's ready to settle on better choices 'consistently.'

This doesn't imply that his choices become more straightforward to make, yet it implies that he has significantly more clearness to settle on better choices. This is significant because if you need to turn into the sort of man that a lady can follow, you must turn out to be amazingly happy with settling on a ton of intense choices that are critical to your life.

Chapter 14: How to Manage Abandonment?

There are only two directions a relationship can go, staying together forever or breakup—but no pressure! Nobody has a crystal ball that tells you when you'll meet your keeper, so it's about dating new people until you do. Unfortunately, not every rejection is so easy to get over, and sometimes a big breakup can be soul-crushing. It can feel like losing your emotional home and mourning the loss of the future you envisioned. Despite that pain, spending too much time chasing after your ex or trying to fix a broken relationship keeps you stuck. For this reason, it's valuable and healthy to know when to call it quits or how to move on when you didn't see the end coming. Let's explore how to cope, heal, and start over without emotional baggage so that you can reopen your heart to more immense and love better.

Feel Your Feelings

As a species, we thrive and survive in close and intimate relationships. A romantic rejection leaves us feeling unprotected, alone, and like we don't matter. When you suffer a romantic loss, you may feel like a zombie walking through a world that has recently collapsed. This may not be what you want to hear, but the best way to get through your uncomfortable emotions is to face them and work through them. Experience these painful feelings. Stop intellectualizing and be with yourself on an emotional level.

I advise clients to do the following exercise: Close your eyes, put one hand over your heart and the other on top of your stomach, take some deep breaths, and then see what emotions bubble up inside you. You may think you know what you're feeling but be surprised at what you find when you sit in silence. It may be rage, remorse, loneliness, devastation, stress, embarrassment, betrayal, shame, or an array of other conflicting emotions, like relief and joy. A brain imaging study performed by psychologists at UCLA shows that when you become mindful of your emotions and identify them, your brain activates the region associated with emotional regulation. This means that you take the first step to gain control over that feeling by assessing and correctly categorizing what you feel.

In contrast, when you don't carve out time to process and label your emotions, your brain doesn't regulate the response you're having, and as a result, you may experience those emotions more intensely. So, observe your emotions in a nonjudgmental way—without labeling them as good or bad. Trust that there's a regular part of you that can hold firm and allow these feelings to flow in and out like waves. You can stay put but recognizing your feelings, but not recognizing them will knock you over entirely. Welcome each emotion rather than resisting them. It may feel silly but speak to the emotions out loud, "Hello, anger. I see you; I feel you; I honor you." Then go about your day without any rash to change it.

When You Choose to End It

Sometimes the person you love breaks your heart. But sometimes you break your own heart—And that's okay. Be courageous and end the relationship when it doesn't feel right. An intuitive way to know that the relationship isn't right is when your head and heart are not aligned. Maybe you can't put your finger on what's wrong or missing, but just the fact that you're torn between your head and heart is essential information. When your heart asks for more or believes that more exists, regard that—even if you don't know what the alternative looks like. If your head is telling you it won't work because it's too complicated, or you find yourself compromising too much, or you're losing yourself in the relationship, believe your head. Not everyone has an instant clarity that they've found their forever person. Relationships can improve with effort and investing in professional assistance. Sometimes you know the relationship isn't right because you find

105

yourself constantly questioning it. Maybe you're always wondering if there's a better match out there, or your love tank still feels empty even when you've learned to speak each other's love languages, or you just feel like you make better friends than lovers. It might be time to walk away. When you're with the right person, your head and heart will agree. Believe that there's a kind of love out there that will clarify why it didn't work out with anyone else.

When the Other Person Ends It

Hold on to your hat because you're about to go for a ride on the roller coaster of grief. There are standard stages of breakup grief through which everyone will eventually pass. The keyword here is eventually, since similar to grieving a death, there's no exact timeline, and everyone copes differently. You'll move through feelings of denial during which you may be in shock that it's over or feel emotionally numb. This is like a survival mode for your mind when your brain and body prepare for a big transition. As your new reality sinks in, you'll experience the stage of bargaining and anxiety, during which you may try to convince your partner to stay with you—making unrealistic promises in an attempt to salvage the relationship. You'll spend a lot of time ruminating and obsessing about what went wrong and missing her. The problem is that the more time you waste begging for your ex to come back, the more you convince yourself that the only way to be happy is with her by your side. However, the one who broke you can't fix you. It's hard, but the best thing you can do is admit to yourself that the relationship was not perfect. If it had been, she would not have chosen to end it.

You'll also likely experience intermittent anger, which could be directed at your ex, yourself, the universe, or even your friends and family for not understanding your pain. Often the thing living underneath anger is a deep hurt. I would be remiss if I did not acknowledge that sometimes this sadness can spiral and include emotional and physical symptoms. You may even feel hopeless about your future. It is normal to feel all of this for days or weeks—depending on how long or severe the relationship was— but if you find that it's going on for months, your sadness over the breakup may have transformed into a more severe depression. If you're struggling with depression, please seek professional help. In addition to this, do your best to take care of yourself by eating healthy food, getting enough sleep, being careful not to abuse substances, and especially by getting some exercise even when you don't feel like it—since doing so releases endorphins and dopamine, which will make you feel a little better.

When you've been broken up with, some of your pain is probably coming from feeling blindsided, a fear of change, the distress of starting over, worrying how others will judge you, or feeling like a failure. The thing is that there are no failures in dating—there are only experiences from which to learn and grow. Think about that: There are no failures. Every relationship ends until you get to the one that doesn't—and you learn things about yourself from each of those relationships—which makes you more equipped for the next one. Your most significant transformation occurs from your lowest low, so even though you're hurting, the meaning you make out of your pain is gold. When you can make this positive reframe, you'll turn your setback into a comeback—and it will be fierce!

One day, you'll feel lighter and as the mental load of these emotions has been taken off your shoulders. You'll reach a place of acceptance that will be the final stage of your grief. Some days you may feel triggered and get sucked right back into the intense earlier stages; however, you'll find that you can more quickly and easily get to the calmer and more contented place of acceptance as time passes. You've made peace with the end of the relationship in the acceptance stage, even if you aren't happy about how the breakup went down. You're optimistic about your love life and what the future could hold. You can get to a place of acceptance once you've forgiven yourself for things such as sticking around for too long or investing time, energy, and finances when it wasn't reciprocated; for continuing to pour love into a taker who didn't give back; for compromising on your core values, ignoring your intuition, lowering your standards, and not honoring yourself while in the relationship. Focus less on trying to grant forgiveness to your ex and ruminating on her behavior and more on being compassionate toward yourself for your transgressions and loving the parts of you that feel shameful. The way to release ill will and resentment and slowly reopen your heart is by embracing love for yourself. Real forgiveness comes when you create space for it, and it takes time to get to that better place. Forgiving your ex doesn't mean you have to maintain or rebuild a friendship or even communicate with her directly.

In most cases, I recommend rigid boundaries, like removing them from social media and no contact, especially at the beginning of the breakup. Eventually, you may get to a place where you can genuinely wish her peace from afar, realizing that people who cause you pain are likely in pain themselves. The reality is that a broken heart is painful and takes time to recover, so be patient and kind to yourself.

No Regrets

When you've been rejected or your heart is broken into a million pieces, it's easy to act irrationally. You may not recognize yourself while sending nasty, hate-fueled e-mails, entering stalker mode driving by their house, creeping on social media to see who they're dating, drunk dialing and leaving voice mails you'll regret in the morning, or maybe double or triple texting when you don't hear back from them, or scheming ways to get revenge. I once had a client who dated a woman. After they split, she called his place of employment and left ranting voice mails for all of the C-level executives about what an asshole he was—all because he didn't want to date her after they'd been sleeping together. Another client's ex-wife poured bleach all over his suits when they divorced. Do your best not to succumb to your worst instincts. These types of behaviors are not healthy. Though acting out may give you instant gratification, behaving with grace during rejection (admittedly easier said than done) will make you feel better in the long run, and preserve your dignity. By behaving irrationally in the face of pain, you're not honoring yourself, and in fact, you are probably confirming to your ex that they made the right choice to let you go. Wouldn't you rather be the one that got away?

When you're hurting, try out the following healthy coping skill backed by science to improve your mood and decrease symptoms of depression and anxiety:

- Call a friend

- Listen to music

- Meditate

- Exercise

- Take a walk in nature

- Color a mandala

- Knit

- Read a book

- Watch something that makes you laugh (like a comedy skit or cat videos on YouTube)

A less scientific—but some would argue equally helpful—approach is to visit your stylist for some hair counseling since a new haircut and color can change your appearance from the person you were in the relationship. This "makeover" will have you walking away feeling lighter, both physically and mentally.

If you're feeling alone, remember to lean on friends who will give you a sense of belonging. Rather than ex-bashing, ask her to tell you about how she noticed you weren't your best self in that relationship. When you're blinded by love, it can be hard to see the relationship for what it was, so your besties can bring a fresh perspective. You may be surprised to see how you didn't value yourself or how you gave away your power when dating your ex.

Or let them distract you with funny stories from their lives that have nothing to do with your ex. Let them be there for you.

Chapter 15: Persuasive Communication in All Social Situations

Influence alludes to the mental impact, which influences the decision that an individual should make. With influence, an individual is regularly disposed to make you purchase their way of thinking by an offer to change your perspective. With the end goal for one to adequately accomplish influence, various things should be placed at the top of the priority list. When we can go past the standard human structure and get a grip of what moves others, at that point, you are in a situation to accomplish a compelling influence. This is because you know about the compel focuses and how best to control them.

To become an alpha male, you have to craft the art of influence, and for that, we have to address different indicators, like the ones below:

Imitating

As a reasonable human being, you probably begin to do things in a certain way and then you change to the next one, which is in this case would be the people you date or fall in love with. But as you change along the way, that could make others think of you as inconsistent. Attributable to this specific certainty, you will find that as people, we tend to be warm and inviting to those individuals who display similar qualities as us. Those qualities may be character-related or behavior-related. This sort of procedure is said to evoke good emotions that may kick in regarding influence. When an individual has the sensation of loving towards somebody, the person in question is in a situation to be influenced by your impact.

In an offer to expand on this specific sort of strategy, we will utilize this situation's utilization. In the inn business, particularly in the most exceptional and top of the line ones, you will find that the host's and servers' treatment is subject to the customer. Excellent quality inns in the business have high client criticism, and accordingly, they will treat their customers in a way that proposes so. A customer, for example, would be apportioned a specific sort of server which coordinates their depiction. For example, French servers are famous for their fantastic assistance. Prioritizing customers is at the first spot on the list. Numerous inn owners have prevailed because of their ability to infer the better way to treat each customer. Placing the customer into thought goes a step higher in stating the specific words that the customer has said. With this, they can suspect that you have suitably decoded what they implied.

To precisely accomplish this specific procedure, an individual should do various things. First, the person may consider doing a top to bottom examination into the specific field of the inquiry to ensure that what is expected of them is met. Before you can accomplish influence by utilizing this method, one should know the person in question should be convinced by you. This kind of skill should be sufficiently sharp to ensure that it evokes significant focuses that may prove useful during the cycle of influence.

Social Proof

With regards to influence, social proof (also known as informational social influence) has more than once demonstrated its predominance. Before we go further into the method, we first need to refer to the importance of social verification. Social proof alludes to the cycle by which a person's emotions and point of view are influenced by how others have responded to a similar issue regarding social impact. A person who is the persuader draw their premise from the demonstrations that others have occupied with consistently. It very well may be the standard. With individuals, the peril that happens is the inclination to be dependent on a gathering of individuals. People need to have a feeling of having a place either in a group or in a particular movement or something, and this is the thing that puts them in more danger of being impacted relatively easily.

Utilizing social proof while convincing an individual will imply that you have a premise of a standard utilized repeatedly by the individuals we consider to be in a similar class. This premise should be something that the vast majority take part in, and not just a few of them. For example, take a person who just started being part of a group. That beginner would, maybe, look at the most experienced or popular ones and start imitating them. Even though they probably won't choose a similar alternative as the remainder of the group in question, this will be relatively developing on to what decision they may decide to settle upon. Or maybe they may wind up grasping what others have utilized. In that particular setting of social proof, the actions and stunts someone would ever do will be aligned with how the person wants to be seen by the members of that group. You will accomplish influence by persuading someone you are in a group with that an enormous that you and the others in the group have grasped the ideal alternative.

Correspondence

In regard to this kind of method, one requirement to comprehend that if a decent deed was done by someone, regardless of how far-off, it will generally go even further ahead to the future while being performed by others. From its phrasing, correspondence alludes to the cycle by which an individual can react to a decent deed by playing out a decent deed consequently. Practicing the latter, you will find that the vast majority neglect to correspond good deeds or even give some sort of feedback, which requires a great deal of commitment. On the planet today, it is nearly as uncommon as the sun ascending from the west, all things considered, to discover somebody who will broaden sensations of warmness and care towards you. Save the individuals you are firmly related to, and you will feel diverse when a person who isn't even in your hover of companionship expresses kind sentiments.

The sensation of commitment can emerge when you are done a good deed by someone else. This is the consequence of being reached out with sensations of warmness. Now, you are in a situation to convince the person in the way that you wish. This is because the person would be obliged to continue toward the breeze. It ought to be noticed that this specific kind of procedure should be done carefully. This is because the ramifications of correspondence don't keep going forever. There are cutoff points to this course of events that shouldn't be surpassed and let alone abused because not having enough time can debilitate the needed correspondence or feedback.

To practice good correspondence, you should commit to offering in ways that are right for the situations in question taking into account the tone or style of the group. On the off chance that your offer is justified, despite all the trouble at that point, it raises a commitment impact over again—making a successful circumstance.

Consistency and Commitment

This kind of procedure is wired on an all-around shaped discernment. When an individual is in a situation to make a specific decision, the decision that this individual picks would be fixed on the person to question the extent to which they go. From its phrasing, consistency and commitment allude to how an individual is trying to settle on a decision and stick to it with sheer assurance and constancy. Regarding influence, not all strategies may work, and you may find that you hit absolute bottom on more than one occasion in your endeavor. At the point when this occurs, it isn't prudent to surrender. Consistency is the thing that assembles our character in pretty much every feature throughout everyday life. Consistency and commitment are of the utmost importance not only in training and business but also in day-to-day life. The primary way to influence a person is through providing motivations instead of just persuading them—if you really want them to wind up in a way that you wish. Persuading somebody is regularly described as dismissal and sometimes mental torment, which should be dealt with by not surrendering to it. The ideal way the deal with situations when people dismiss your opinions is by making sure that you have a group of other people who comprehends what you are saying.

The discussion of consistency and commitment is one that doesn't go down the throat without any problem. This is because these are the most inconspicuous features to grasp since they will, in general, affect the way a person lives. You can envision being dismissed severally. To have commitment, an individual should work continually.

Chapter 16: Seduction Through Social Media

Do you think you know what it takes to find a good woman online? Online is a lot more complicated than it is in person as it removes some of the things that could be used as an advantage by a man, like the use of touch.

You should not only know how to talk to her using a particular technique, but you should also know how to present yourself appropriately online using your pictures, user profile, and even your e-mail.

Gaining knowledge of those techniques substantially increases your luck in finding a good woman on the internet.

If you want to know some of the tips to gain all this success, don't fret, because tips are listed below:

Secret #1: Highlight Your Strengths

Online dating, if you aren't informed already, consists of your picture, your name, and something that you to show to the website to lure women into striking a conversation in hopes that you may share an interest and start dating.

You will notice that in most of the men's profiles they tend to... 'Knock their esteem down.' These men, instead of introducing themselves in a way that may appear appealing to a woman, start their descriptions by:

"Hi, I am Michael Duncan, also known as Mr. Lonely... blah blah blah."

I am not sure what is going through their minds and why they consider that something appealing for women. DO NOT DO THAT AT ALL COSTS.

If you want to be successful in online dating, you need to 'highlight your strength' or in other words, you need to make sure you display yourself as a powerful and sexually attractive man in the least boastful way possible.

By doing this, you will be on top of the need-to-date list of any dating site.

First and foremost, in becoming a master online dater, you must display strength. Simply ask yourself, "What do I have that women want."

It is hard to evaluate yourself without seeming cocky, so here are two secrets:

- **Secret #1:** Find out what women find attractive about you. Ask this during dates and find out your best features.
- **Secret #2:** Think back to the positive aspects of your features or personality that people have said to you before.

Both allow you to grow knowledge on the areas you need to improve on—more than those that people have said you should keep because it adds to your attraction.

The strategy of 'highlighting your strengths' is to exhibit your best features and your strengths.

Combine it with picturing her as a future of a perfect romantic life that would make her giggle and feel butterflies against the less lively life she is living in right now.

Doing this not only shows her that you are a man that knows the type of man he is meant to be, but this also shows her that you can take her to a whole new world through experiencing life in a whole new light.

Communicating with women like this will intensify their attraction to you and make them WANT to be with you.

Try it out; the results will be stunning.

Secret #2: Confidence Is the Key!

Every man has a few, if not many, attributes or features that attract women.

The problem is that, usually, men with attractive features have no idea that they have those features and don't know how to use them.

To be that 'confident' alpha male you want to be, don't start describing yourself with weak sentences such as, "I'm not sure, but people say..." or "I like to think I am..."

Instead of this, you need to learn to describe yourself in striking and straightforward terms—in terms that would show the woman that you are a confident man.

Make sure not to exaggerate; however, be aware not to appear cocky.

There's a psychological study that says, "If you can talk about your strengths rather than your weaknesses, so will everyone too."

Do you want some proof of this?

Do you think Lyle Lovett, who isn't exactly considered a model, captured Julia Roberts by focusing on his physical features? Not entirely, Lyle also focused on other qualities, such as his confidence and charm, which was what Julia Roberts perceived him to be and not his 'odd resemblance to 'Shrek' that he so kindly states.

Once you learn to live with your strengths and not your weaknesses, women will take notice of that and take on the impression that you're a man of confidence and strength. Just the man any woman would be interested in.

Secret #3: Display Some Mystery

In online dating, men usually think it's good to display their qualities straight in the description—saying that they are doctors or travelers or even helpers of the orphanage.

Do you know what this does? It throws away the mystery that you display on your profile. You have already instantly given away a label. You will lose the woman's interest in doing so because the woman would have known all she had to know about you and could judge you before even talking to you.

If you can describe yourself in a way, that may not be saying much but just enough for her to get intrigued, then that's the type of description you're going for.

Curiosity killed the cat... and will also lure the woman in.

Secret #4: Exhibit Sensuality

Women want to know that men can appreciate the sense of 'touch' as much as women do and that they can create and stir in intoxicatingly passionate feelings inside her.

How do you do this, you say? It would be wildly assuming and rude to go into a straightforward and direct approach like saying, "I know how to make women feel good"; you need to master the ability to make her feel good while you are communicating with her.

Simple tip: Use vivid details. If a man was to discuss wine, you don't just say, 'I like fine wine.' No. That's boring. You need to explain how much you love the feel and texture of how it tastes in your mouth or talking about a nice, relaxed walk on the beach, you will lose her interest by saying, "Yeah, you know, I like walks on the beach." Stop right there and describe how you love the feel of the sand between your toes or the feel of the ocean as it swims by.

I suggest you use words like tender, warm, supple, etc. By using words like this, you provide power to her imagination by suggesting the subject of sex, which will send a message to her senses. She will feel aroused without even touching you. This is what she wants to hear and how she wants to hear it.

Secret #5: Electrify Your Life

What most guys don't seem to get is that if you want an interesting woman, then you must attract her interest by doing exciting things.

Here's an example of that type of situation:

You meet this girl you are interested in, and you have come to know her as someone adventurous, but unfortunately, you have never done anything remotely adventurous in your life.

How do you think you will be able to communicate with her on her level?

If you want to be able to be with someone as impressive as that, then you need to get up and DO something interesting. There are a million exciting things you could do.

Go hiking! Go diving off a cliff! Swim with sharks!

If you can experience things like these, you will understand her on her level of experience and you will both have a commonality.

Suppose you don't have the time, money, or aren't in a remote and exciting area, in that case, you can be interesting in other ways, like taking classes that you are interested in and maybe she might find it interesting too...

Some good options are art classes, cooking classes, or even just educating yourself through reading stories. Women will be amazed by your abilities in these activities.

Men would usually think that participating in these classes would be embarrassing, and they would hide in fear of that, but if women realize that you're going out of your way to improving yourself and who you are as a person, then you are on the right track to a womanizer.

Even simple things, like mentioning things you've done in the past, like going to an art exhibit or reading a cooking book for a while, would show her that you want to keep improving continually.

Women are all about that and they will be all over you too...

Secret #6: Push Her "Buttons"

Women appreciate it when men can communicate well and talk to them directly about their wants, needs, desires, and life goals.

She will feel a real connection if you can understand her in this manner.

Now, there are wrong buttons in talking to women, but there are also right buttons.

You see a woman on the dating website mention in her description box that she likes children.

"An example of a wrong button merely is e-mailing her that you love children too. All men say this, and honestly, this makes no impact at all towards her." Nil. Nada.

The right button to push is that, instead of going directly to the interest, you need to approach it subtly; you can do this by saying how you miss and loved the times when you would come home and play hide-and-seek with your baby cousins all afternoon.

If you don't think that'll attract her attention, I don't know what will.

Or if a woman was talking about how she has a great relationship with her mom, don't approach it by saying, "Yeah, I love my mom too." You approach this in a way that you loved to see your mom smile when you surprised her one morning with pancakes and syrup.

Do you get the picture I'm trying to paint for you?

You need to approach this in a way that demonstrates, in your experiences, that you can relate to the things she finds vital.

That would create an instant connection between both of you. And by that time, she will probably want to meet this charming man—who loves his mother so much—in person.

Secret #7: Tell Good Stories Well

Being able to tell a great story won't only be successful with women, but it will also help make friends—or your future kids at bedtime!

Chapter 17: The Power of Mental Programming

There are different ways which people use to control the minds of others. Given below are some of these techniques.

Subliminal Messaging

These are either visual or auditory messages sent to a receiver's brains to bypass the person's everyday conscious perceptions. To do this effectively, the mind controller flashes these messages to the other person's brain without giving the person's eyes the chance to capture/see the image or by making sounds inaudible for the receiver's ears.

The messages are sent directly to the brain. The mind controller aims to influence the other person, and they do that effectively using this technique.

Brainwave Synchronization

For everything a person does or thinks, there is a group of neurons that communicate with each other in the brain. These neurons generate and transmit electrical signals between themselves, creating patterns in waves known as brainwaves. For different states of mind of a person, there are different resultant frequencies of these brainwaves.

Thus, the question becomes whether it is possible to get to a predetermined state of mind.

Neuro-Linguistic Programming (NLP)

This is a technique that has its basis in the idea that successful behavioral patterns can be made possible in either oneself or other people by modifying underlying thought patterns and interpersonal relationships or interactions.

Cognitive-Behavioral Therapy

This is a therapeutic technique that may not be related to mind control but works perfectly when it comes to the underlying principle of modifying a person's behavior, known as behavioral modification, based on corresponding thought modification.

Hypnosis

This is a mind-control tool used by professional hypnotists to fish out a person's suggestible subconscious mind by moving past the conscious and analytical mind, creating positive thoughts, or replacing old negative beliefs that the mind has held onto for a long time.

Manipulating the Mind with NLP

As you may already know, several techniques can be employed when it comes to mind control.

Pay Close Attention to the Person

When a person is trying to manipulate another person's mind using NLP, they do so by first paying close attention to the subtle cues of the person like breathing pattern, body language, pupil dilation, eye movement, nervous tics, body flushes, and so on. Thanks to the fact that a person's emotions are easily linked to such cues, it is easy for the NLP user to infer the person's state of mind.

Talking with a Suggestive Frequency of the Human Mind

This has to do with uttering words close to a person's heartbeat, typically about 42 to 72 beats per minute. When this is done, it can induce a high state of suggestibility into a person's mind.

Moving Past the Conscious Mind with the Use of Voice Roll

This is a manipulating technique that has to do with voice roll, a patterned pace style that get's to the desired point by skipping a person's conscious mind and going to the subconscious mind. An NLP practitioner does this by emphasizing the word they desire the receiver to hear in a patterned style of monotony.

Building Rapport in Secret Easily

This is a manipulative technique used by the skilled NLP practitioner. It is done by employing language to boost suggestibility. To create a rapport with a person, the NLP professional examines the person closely and pretends to adopt the person's body language subtly, making the person more vulnerable to everything the NLP practitioner suggests.

Programming the Mind in A Sublime Manner

This technique has to do with creating an anchor in a person in such a way that it becomes easy to put the person in a particular state of mind by merely tapping on the person or touching them to program the person's mind sublimely.

Using Hot Words in an Effective Way

NLP professionals can adopt a pattern of words that may seem normal on the surface but are permissive and suggestive in truth. Some hot words are connected to the senses. These are the more suggestive ones.

They include "eventually," "feel free," "see this," "means," "hear this," "now," "because," "as," etc. These words are very potent in invoking a state of mind, like experiencing, feeling, imagining, etc. It also creates the perception that the NLP practitioner desires in the mind of a person. They can also make use of some vague words to control a person's thoughts.

Interpersonal Subconscious Mind Programming

Using an interpersonal strategy, the NLP practitioner can say one thing when planting something else in their subject's subconscious mind.

Protecting Oneself from NLP Mind Control

Many times, whether you are conscious of it or not, people will try to use NLP mind control on you to have you become submissive to them. This will include those you work with and those you get into intimate relationships with. However, developing a keen and potent immunity to it will be of much help to you.

To do this, you must closely study the mechanics that are employed by experts in the field. Jason Louv (N.D.) suggests the following as ways of protecting oneself from NLP mind control.

Worry of Those Who Copy Your Body Language

When you are talking to a person that you suspect may be into NLP, and you note that they are trying to copy some of your gestures and mannerisms by either trying to sit the way you sit or trying to place their hands the way you have placed yours, put them to test by making a few adjustments to the way you sit and by changing the way you have placed some parts of your body to see if they will do the same.

Make Random Movements with Your Eyes

You will find that this is a hilarious way to troll NLP freaks, but you should try it out for what it's worth, especially when your rapport with the NLP person is at its initial stage. At this stage, they will generally try their best to pay keen attention to your eyes. You may be deceived into thinking that their attention to your eyes is because they are interested in what you have to say.

Avoid Being Touched by Anyone

This may be an evident practice, but it should be done with more caution when you have a conversation with a person you suspect may be into NLP.

This is an essential practice whenever you find yourself in a heightened emotional state of anger, laughter, or anything like that. The person you are having a conversation with attempts to touch you at a point when you are still in that state.

For example, they may choose to tap you on the shoulder. If they did this, they would have successfully anchored you so that if they desire to make you go back to that state after, they can just touch you on the same spot. This is as suggested by NLP wayward logic.

Chapter 18: The Alpha Male and Differences from Others

Each man has a kind character attribute that makes him what he is and characterizes his activities. Despite apparently irregular acts and methods of going about existence being the standard for all men, there are approaches to classify a man's activities into more explicit attributes and inclinations.

The male character classification below will assist us with seeing how and why a man carries on with his life, the way he does. We should perceive what every one of these six novel characters offers by noticing their four most common characteristics.

The Alpha Male

He Is Confident

The expression "alpha male" is a term the vast majority know, and for a valid justification. The expression "alpha male" begins from all animals' set, portraying the highest point of the pack. Because of this arrangement, the alpha male usually is going to be optimistic about how he acts and approaches his life. Certainty is the capacity to go into a wide cluster of circumstances and realize that you will endure regardless of how unfriendly the circumstances are.

Certainty is not a characteristic human inclination, and even an alpha male character type gets sure over the long haul.

He Is Outgoing

The certainty that an alpha male has is evident from a long way off. This implies he can communicate with pretty much anybody, and he permits his likable character to help him throughout everyday life. An alpha male is unshaken when moving toward a man or lady, as he has the right stuff and appeals to converse with anybody.

If an alpha male needs to converse with somebody, nothing can hinder him. Being cordial permits the alpha male to make more social associations and structure associations with more noteworthy productivity than other character types.

He Is a Leader

When somebody is asked to lead the pack on a venture at work, it is the alpha character who assumes responsibility and administration. Numerous fruitful men on the planet are viewed as alpha guys since they are anxious to lead others and have the stuff to request that others follow them on their excursion.

Alpha guys make such great leaders since they are generally rousing to other people who are happy to follow them. An alpha male realizes how to get a group to cooperate to achieve an objective.

He Is Charismatic

Moxie is an attribute that an alpha male radiates with almost all that he does. Magnetism is the appeal of a man whom everybody needs to know. Magnetic men act like a James Bond type of character, as they act and talk as indicated by their principles.

The magnetism that alpha guys transmit is an essential explanation as to why people flock around them. An alluring individual is amusing to be near and will typically be mainstream with the individuals looking for satisfaction from life.

The Beta Male

He Is Friendly

With a great deal of antagonism encompassing the beta male character, we need to comprehend that this fundamental character type isn't anything to be embarrassed about. A beta male is a man who isn't a weakling or somebody to peer down on but rather somebody who is inviting and regards others.

Being cordial is a reason why numerous individuals partner with the beta male character. Whether it is towards a man or a lady, the beta male needs to be inviting and kind to everybody, and he will pick up others' endorsement and adoration.

He Is Reserved

One of the fundamental qualities related to beta guys is being reserved. This standard reservation is the thing that leads individuals to think a beta male is modest and not ready to impart his insights. While the facts confirm that some beta guys are modest, many are only hesitant to transparently impart their insights.

The journaling of the beta male is something that drives them to dodge numerous social associations. Being reserved doesn't imply that beta guys don't talk much; however, it implies that they are restricted in how much impact their words or thoughts can have.

He Is Submissive

A mark average for the beta male is being accommodated and attempting to try not to offend anyone. Being accommodating implies that when a beta male faces judgment or assessment, the beta males will probably try not to shield himself if this implies that the other individual will detest him.

While many views are compliant as a negative attribute, there are times when being agreeable has its advantages. If somebody is merely attempting to contend with you or stir up some dust, being compliant regularly causes that person to lose interest and keeps the beta male safe.

He Is Loyal

The last characteristic for the beta male, and perhaps the greatest strength, is that he is exceptionally faithful. One motivation behind why the beta male is an excellent companion is that he is faithful to the individuals who regard him and are inviting.

The devotion of beta guys likewise makes them incredible representatives, since they will probably manage their responsibilities and not intrude on the general work process structure. The beta male may not generally express his real thoughts. However, he will consistently be by his companions' side when he is required.

The Gamma Male

He Is Adventurous

The gamma male is an intriguing character. He is viewed as having a smidgen of all other types of man consolidated as a part of his character—with no particular one of those characters being predominant. One of the primary advantages of this is that the gamma male is brave throughout everyday life and makes his way away from others' assessments.

The alpha male acts in a manner that satisfies others, but he will also do anything he desires to feel satisfied in his life.

He Is Eager

The gamma male will probably be an individual who is anxious to get numerous things throughout everyday life. In favor of involvement and appreciating what the world has to bring to the table, the gamma male will probably need to attempt new things and be anxious to learn new abilities.

He Is Aware

What helps the gamma male stand out from the crowd is his capacity to know about his activities and how they influence others. This can likewise be his vital aspect of getting much of anywhere in his life.

He Is Empathetic

Compassion has generally been viewed as a female characteristic, so observing a man's demonstration with a feeling of empathy is intriguing and maybe somewhat atypical. The compassion experienced by a gamma male permits him to comprehend what others are experiencing to go about as such an emotionally supportive figure for other people.

The Omega Male

He Is Self-Guaranteed

The alpha male depends on his gathering for the consolation of his character and status; the omega male acts differently from that, with little respect for how others see him. Along these lines, the omega male's self-appreciation affirmation permits him to maintain a strategic distance from insignificant challenges.

He Is Driven

With so much inner capacity to push him ahead, you will probably see an omega male being headed to do what he needs. He is his own best team promoter and will give himself all the inspiration he requires to make a move or prevail at finishing an undertaking.

He Is Intelligent

The standard "geek" prime example is something you can see among omega guys, as they are exceptionally centered around insight and learning. An omega male is somebody who can move through complex calculations and equations to figure out a code that others are regularly unable to comprehend.

He Has Diversified Interests

Obliging is the somewhat geeky focal point of omega guys. They are regularly locked in with computer games and dark leisure activities. Things that invigorate his psyche like structure models and side interests are precisely what an omega male couldn't imagine anything better to invest energy and time in.

The Delta Male

He Is Resigned

The delta male offers a unique perspective on how an individual can change a character type. The delta male typically has experienced an encounter that has made him change into a delta male. Whatever the experience might be, a delta male will turn out to be more reserved as a result of it.

He Is Resentful

Going close by their exciting past that has made them not draw near other people, delta guys frequently hold some measure of hatred towards others. The delta male will seldom search internally to determine issues as he seeks others to fault for his issues.

He Is Self-Attacking

The delta male frequently does not have the truth of life that you need to manage yourself regularly. By accusing others of his issues, the delta male will self-damage himself by living under the dream that there isn't anything he can do to live better.

He Is Lonely

The delta male is probably going to be a lonely individual. While he may have once been the inspiration and that everyone needed, the delta male has transformed into something terrible. In allowing himself to get disdainful towards others and losing restraint, the dejection sets in.

The Sigma Male

He Is Cunning

You ought to be wary of sigma guys, as they can simply persuade you regarding something that no one else could. They don't share the intense presence of an alpha male, yet they can simply get their route because of their monstrous tricks and capacity to control individuals and circumstances.

He Is Self-Certain

Similar to his ability to a social circumstance and the individuals in it, the sigma male—where it counts—has no interest in others' assessments. Sigma guys are undoubtedly famous with others. However, they needn't bother with the endorsement of others to feel better and consoled about themselves.

He Is Likable

These sorts of men are frequently going to connect with the alpha and omega characters, as they would all be able to get along at the top in their particular manners. The sigma male's amiability and creative activities are sufficient to regularly get him in whatever gathering or circumstance he needs to be.

He Is Calculating

The last bit of the sigma male character is his capacity to take determined actions and choices with incredible exactness. He will regularly stop before responding to questions to concoct an articulate or amusing explanation if the circumstance calls for it.

Chapter 19: The Relationship You Need to Build with Willpower

In any endeavor you choose to undertake in this life, there will be a necessity to build and utilize a relationship with one crucial skill in particular. This skill is willpower. Willpower is your ability to use your strength to overcome short-term desires or temptations to achieve your long-term goals. There are many ways to describe this crucial skill, but there is one thing for sure and certain. Willpower is your effort to get what you want due to a situation rather than what you want at the moment, which is strikingly difficult for many.

One widespread event that occurs for many people that exemplifies what happens when a person underutilizes their willpower is procrastination. About twenty percent of the population identify themselves as procrastinators, and researchers think that even more people are guilty of consistently procrastinating completing tasks—from substantial pursuits to small. Incredibly, among students, that number leaps to between eighty-five to ninety-five percent! This includes students from all levels of academia—including undergraduate and graduate-level university students. Unfortunately, it correlates with higher self-reported stress levels, a higher rate of illness, and lower grades for procrastinating students, which doesn't sound much like the path to success includes procrastination.

Procrastination acts as the inverse or the opposite of willpower. Willpower is doing what must be done at the moment even if it comes with a (pain point) painful implication or a necessary 'cost' to gain in the long-term and reach a goal, and procrastination is putting off what must be done at the moment, pushing the pain point or 'cost' further down the road; it decreases the present pain point or "cost" by transferring it to the future, often setting up for a loss in the long-term and a failure to reach the goal. By better understanding this inverse of willpower, you can more easily understand how to flip it around and strengthen your willpower.

Mostly, procrastination occurs due to a feeling or impulse to avoid some form of pain or discomfort. For example, students may procrastinate writing a ten-page essay because they know it will be mentally taxing, or a business executive may procrastinate and put off filling out tedious paperwork because they know it will be boring and uninteresting.

Looking back, we've covered how to cultivate mental toughness, and this is a perfect example of why that characteristic is crucial in building the self-discipline skills you need to succeed in your endeavors. To kick procrastination to the curb, you have to be willing to flex your uncomfortable muscles and sit in the discomfort of whatever the situation is, even though you wanting to procrastinate.

You can practice flexing your uncomfortable muscles to override your procrastination impulses by engaging in a fruitful internal dialogue with yourself. For example, say you come home from work every day at five o'clock to feed the cat, and then lo and behold, instead of heading out for a quick jog as you always plan to do, you instead find other things that you suddenly feel that must be done before your jogging. Maybe you tell yourself that you really ought to go ahead and clean the litter box then, or maybe you remember that your sister called you earlier in the day, and you really should go ahead and call her back right now. Still, whatever it is that you are putting before your goal—in this case, your evening jog—is acting as a procrastination obstacle, and you need to get a handle on that because most people will use those obstacles as a convenient roadblock to their goa, "Oops, looks like it is too late to head out for my jog now!"

You can structure an effective internal dialogue with yourself by practicing the events' sequence ahead of time in your mind. Maybe on your drive home, you can visualize yourself walking in your front door, tossing your keys on the entryway table, bending over to pet the top of your cat's head while telling him that you will feed him quickly before your jogging, and then continue talking about heading out for the jog. Narrating your actions can help you feel as if you are being monitored by someone else and you will be accountable for your procrastination if you let other things get in the way of your goal. While you are narrating your actions, keep your tone and vocabulary light and upbeat. You will motivate yourself to complete the tasks you need to complete if you are talking about them as if they are not terrible chores to be avoided.

Willpower is the ability to flip that switch from avoidance of life's pain points to a state in which you willingly embrace them. The relationship you have with your willpower will be very integral in how effective you are with it. If you view your willpower as weak or something that must be fought, you are essentially setting yourself up for failure. If you believe your willpower is weak, you believe you have an inefficient tool for your projects. If you believe your willpower is your enemy, you will waste valuable energy and resources in 'fighting' this enemy.

To reframe and revamp your relationship with your willpower, you will need to shift the way you think of it. Instead of viewing it as something that must be pitied or fought, instead, view it as something that must be tended to carefully. Imagine your willpower as a seed you've just planted in your garden. You wouldn't dig a hole, place the seed in, cover it, and then start complaining about why nothing has happened, right? Of course not! You would understand that you had completed an essential step in planting the seed but now you must continue to ensure that your seed has the right environment to grow and thrive. Your seed will not grow if it does not get enough water, nor will it grow if it gets too much. Your seed must be cared for and paid attention to.

Just as your seed requires your care and attention, so does your willpower. You have to set yourself up for success using tools such as the visualization and self-talk above. Your relationship with your willpower must be healthy and strong. You will not build this skill by shouting at yourself to complete a task or by hoping to 'wing it.' Willpower is a muscle that must be built with repetition and consistency, and as you continue to work on your muscle, it will grow and become stronger. Throughout this process, it will be easier to rely on this muscle to do this vital work, but until then, you will need to continue to work on it in ways that support it and yourself.

Your relationship with your willpower should not be a battle. It should be a partnership, and it will require your careful attention and respect. Continue to cultivate and care for this relationship throughout your life and remember to set yourself up for success

151

by protecting against procrastination—using visualization tools and positive self-talk to keep your willpower seed well-watered and well-fed. Eventually, this seed will grow and your willpower muscles will be strong enough to carry you through on the essential tasks you have as you continue to reach for your goals.

Willpower is the power to do the things you must do to reach your dreams. Don't let your relationship with it falter.

Chapter 20: Methods to Overcome Fear in Any Situation

Fear is the feeling you encounter when you think about a person or something that might harm you. When you experience fear, you get the urge to get away or avoid the threat.

As an emotion, fear is evoked in you when there is a concrete threat to or within your environment. For instance, the mere thought of a fast-approaching car or a spider that crawls over your arm can lead to the feeling of fear in you.

Fear is characterized by things that haven't happened yet—it is about what will happen in the future.

There are so many threats that can evoke fear in you; these include:

- The threat of getting harmed
- Loss of financial or material possessions
- Being afraid to say the wrong thing
- Loss of friendship or closeness
- Hurting other people
- Fear of embarrassment

- Fear of loneliness
- Fear of disgust

Usually, fear is evoked when you get into a situation that will evoke any of the emotions that have been described before.

When you experience fear, you will become occupied by the threat source and look for a way to avoid or escape it. There are immediate threats that will make you react suddenly, but there will also be threats that will make you want to be more cautious.

When the system is working the right way, it will prevent you from getting into dangerous situations, but it will harm you if cross the line.

Things That You Need to Know About Fear

Feeling afraid shouldn't always be seen as bad. Before you can look at the various ways to overcome fear, we need to look at a few things about fear itself.

Fear Can Be Healthy

Feeling fear is one of the ways to keep your brain working usually. When you don't show any fear when faced with a threat, people will see that you have a problem with your body system. Reacting to fear makes you human, and it proves to others that you have your emotions in check.

It Comes in Various Intensities

Fear is an unpleasant experience that ranges from mild to a highly intense level. Mild fear can be from waiting for the results of a test you have done, and intense fear can be news about an accident that involved someone close to you.

Some intense fear can be imprinted into your mind and will require the help of a professional. Constant mild fear, however, will lead to serious harm to your mental and physical health with time.

It Isn't Automatic

Fear may be threefold, coming partly from learning, instinct, and thought. Some of the fears are innate—meaning that they come from your innermost being and you are born with them. The fear of pain is all about survival. The instinct to survive is all about fearing that you might end up dying or getting debilitated when you feel the pain.

Other types of fear are learned. This means that you learn with time to be afraid of particular places and people. When you were born, you never knew that those places existed, but with time you learned that they aren't the best places to go to.

Some fears are taught. For instance, your culture tells you that some people need to be feared and others are not feared. Some animals are meant to be feared while others are revered.

You Don't Need to Be in a Dangerous Situation to Experience Fear

At times, you don't have to be in the presence of a physical threat to experience fear. Fear can be partly due to your thoughts, and since you have been told so many stories about something, you end up relating it to something else that might be nonexistent.

At times, we experience fear due to our imaginations that lead us into thinking of what could happen.

We are most fearful because we have to think, learn, and come up with fear in our minds. At times fear turns into chronic anxiety that arises from nothing at all.

Fear Dictates What You Do Next

When you experience fear, you will freeze, run, fight, or just get frightened.

Freezing means you stop all you are doing and focus on the threat to decide what to do then. For instance, when you get a message that people will be laid off in the company that you work in.

When you evaluate the situation, the next thing is for you to fight or run. If the threat is manageable, you can decide to handle it head-on, but you will decide to run when the fear is too overwhelming.

At times, you neither fight nor flee. You experience the emotion of fear and you take no action at all. However, maintaining a constant state of fright makes you depressed.

How Does Fear Affect the Way, You Function?

Well, the main aim of fear as an emotion is to help you avoid dangerous situations. And just because most of the things that we are afraid of today aren't so life-threatening, the body's response does more harm than good. Let us look at how these emotions affect the way we behave, eventually.

Flight-or-Fight

We have seen the different ways your body responds to threats in the past paragraphs, and we don't need to repeat them here. All we need to do is emphasized that your body reacts to threats in various ways to make sure you get away from the threat as fast as possible.

Failure to Make Rational Decisions

When your stress levels rise due to the fear that you experience, you will realize that the body diverts most of its energy to the limbs, and when you are afraid, you fail to make rational decisions.

When you experience fear, your brain doesn't turn on the risk-taking functions necessary to make rational decisions. What happens then is that you won't assess all the options before you make a decision.

This is why you shouldn't force anyone to make big decisions when they are in a situation where they are afraid. They won't be able to think of their options at all.

Everything Turns Negative

When you are faced with a threat, the brain perceives anything and everything around you to be negative. You will associate the buildings, environment, and anything else within the vicinity to be negative even if they aren't.

How to Conquer Your Fear?

When you keep on ignoring your fear, it grows to chronic proportions. When you decide to face it, it will shrink.

At the start of the year, people come up with resolutions, which are goals that they desire to achieve during the year. Many of them fail while others make it. For those that fail, the main reason is that they fear that they won't make it. This prevents them from achieving what they are after, even if they can succeed.

Ways to Overcome Your Fear

Understand Fear Then Embrace It

Fear is there to keep us safe as we avoid harm. Fear cannot be inherently good or bad, but it serves as a tool for us to make decisions.

Fear has its good and bad sides, so make sure that you take advantage of the right side and learn from fear's destructive effects. You can embrace fear so that it helps you learn lessons but don't let out to control what you do.

Don't Be in a Hurry

When you are faced with a threat, you need to have a plan in mind on how to deal with it. Don't just stand there and wait for something to happen. Instead, you need to come up with a plan and explore your options.

One of the things you need to do is understand what you have at hand to use against the perceived threat. Many undertakings have been ruined because they failed to decide based on what they had at hand. When fear strikes, you should take time to consider whether the right action is to jump to the first thought that comes to your mind or to analyze the various options and make the right decision.

Identify the Fear

When you are faced with a threat, try and understand what kind of fear you are experiencing. Sometimes the mere act of stating what the fear is and then giving it a name will give you the strength you need to deal with it.

Give the fear a name and a size. The size is just the intensity, and it tells you how extensive the fear is so that you can decide whether you can handle it or not. The bigger the fear, the harder it will be for you to handle it.

Remember, when you try to ignore fear, it grows to unmanageable proportions, but it will become smaller when you decide to face it.

Think Long Term

If you are a worker, you might think that you won't be available the next month in the same position. This is too short a time to start worrying about issues; at times, you need to focus your brain on long-term solutions so that you reduce the fear of the unknown.

When you think about a long-term goal, you won't fix the short-term issues, but it will allow you to think about stuff on a more objective scale and develop the perfect solution.

Educate Yourself

No one is as afraid of anything more than of what they don't know. If your fear comes from a lack of information, then it is the right time to get the information you want to get the fear out of the picture.

Take time to understand what fear is all about, then go ahead to know how you can handle it the right way. There are various ways to get this information, including online blogs, research papers, books, and more.

Be Prepared

When you had a negative experience with something and failed to handle it the right way, you need to get prepared so that you won't have to react negatively again.

Many people have the innate fear of standing in front of people and saying something. If you fear your performance in a particular aspect, you need to prepare for the task well before facing the fear again.

Utilize the Push of Peer Pressure

If you have had a phobia for some time, it is usually good to have a few friends around to help you overcome it.

Have you ever done something scary, like parachuting out of a flying plane just because you had your friends there to push you to do it?

Peer pressure can be good or bad; it only depends on how the pressure is used.

Chapter 21: Improving Focus

To improve your concentration and fixation throughout everyday life, be careful. Care is, without judgment, a second-by-second consciousness of sensations, sentiments, and contemplations. It is a delicate acknowledgment of anything coming into your mindfulness without needing to pass judgment.

Care allows you to venture back, easing back the down-cycle. It gives a feeling of importance to ordinary errands. Note that there are no obvious or right answers with care; it's about your mindfulness and the undiluted experience of living.

Discovering Focus and Concentration

"I realized how to focus," you might say. At the point when the vision turns out to be clear, separating explicit objectives or goals is more enthusiastically. The capacity to zero in is conceivable, and the cycle of progress turns out to be more agreeable to control or rehash.

The level of concentration and focus of proficient competitors at the highest point of their game is something very similar to that of guardians, mentors, instructors, specialists, real estate professionals, specialists, communicators, and so forth. They share the view that it is never the glitches, the mishaps, or the mistakes that keep an individual down, but instead the messages that a person tells themselves. Stuff will happen to you, but you need to respond to those things in a controlled way and decide whether to get away from or go through the situation to overcome it.

Many individuals don't believe that they are running their lives. And others accept that their life is controlling them.

Giving up is tied in with moving somewhere else and settling on a conscious choice. We don't give up by saying, "I would prefer not to discuss it." It resembles checking out the very thing we need to stop with a yellow marker. Consider an instructor saying, "Alright, kids, don't dream of a dark gorilla with enormous orange eyes fluttering in the air." Even if you planned to relinquish it, there's a simple approach to relinquish it. We direct our concentration toward something different and continue putting our psyche precisely where we need it to be until the cerebrum gets the message. So, remember that we are responsible for and in charge of our lives. It's our time. Consider permitting these impediments and difficulties to do only a specific something: Fill in as a suggestion to ponder and focus on those considerations and issues that we can take care of, and on those things that have importance for themselves.

Kindly Do the Meetings

One approach to build up consistency in consideration and focus is to utilize unwinding procedures and, much better, self-spellbinding.

If you quiet your brain—quieting your body is acceptable, yet loosening up your psyche is the key to greatness—you may have numerous interruptions. Work on guiding the thoughtfulness regarding those demonstrations and aptitudes that you need, for example, to adapt rapidly with definitive agreement, to give clear clarifications that are guided, to be propelled by the excusal and undermining procedures of others, to investigate with trust, to experience a memory that can undoubtedly get to pictures and data that serve, to play brief, dependable, golf, to be quiet and agreeable. Feeling "genuine" or "right now" isn't only an articulation. In giving up, they are characteristics that can be dominated and refined on a phenomenal method to perform.

Ask Yourself the Million-Dollar Inquiry

Another method of rehearsing the advancement of concentration and focus is to ask yourself the entire day, "Is the thing that I'm doing the most helpful thing I can do at present?" Write questions in a 3x5-inch card to do the inquiry and carry it with you for half a month to give you energy and a feeling of authority throughout your day. On the off chance that the answer is "Totally," attempt to do what you're doing. On the off chance that the appropriate response is "No," focus and make a move that pushes you NOW to utilize all your time, energy, and assets.

The beginning of any change cycle might be disorderly and terrible. Nonetheless, it's justified, despite all the trouble as well. Take a gander at the individuals you think "have it all," and you may note that they are not the most skilled or splendid ones.

Command Triumphs

Instead of believing in life as a turn of events, you can see it as things that happen as a result of the conviction, determination, confidence, and actions of people that take charge of themselves. Start any place you are and show yourself what you can do. At the point when you accomplish something admirably, stay away from the snare of reasoning, "It is anything but a serious deal." Recognize triumphs, little or monstrous, as being of equivalent worth comparative with your capacity to succeed. What's minuscule to you can be huge to another person and the other way around. The celebration of each accomplishment, paying little heed to its size, keeps on pushing us ahead.

Here are three different ways in which you can improve your memory execution by improving your concentration abilities.

Each Thing in Turn

It is enticing to perform different activities at the same time in the assumption of being more gainful. Regardless, a few examinations have indicated that performing various tasks hurts and is exceedingly awful for our memory. It is fundamental to zero in on each thing in turn to improve your work memory.

The human cerebrum is fantastic. However, it can just oblige each flood of thought in turn. The conviction that we can ingest numerous thoughts is just a brain-exhausting idea—brain damage instead of concentration. This drastically defers memory stockpiling and recovery. Another approach to improving concentration is to part the time and space into accessible pieces during which each task is finished and each memory is stored. However, in case you're not used to this, it very well may be challenging to track. Another approach to implementing this consistency is by utilizing a clock.

The key tips are:

- Decide on the mission to be done.
- Clear the contrary arrangement of your natural world and PC work areas.

- Avoid Interruptions. Switch off your cellphones or email warnings and tell companions and partners not to interrupt you.
- Set your alarm clock on a specific hour.
- Please execute this capacity until the clock is off.
- Take a short 3-5-minute break and rehash.

Contemplation for Focus and Self-Discipline

If you are not engaged or self-restrained, attempt contemplation. Genuine reflection is a remedy to outrage, narcissism, and interruptions. Reflection is a focused movement that numerous individuals battle with. Your body would not like to sit still and think. Your body is more attracted to a few little guilty pleasures. Be that as it may, if you are set up to contemplate and inhale, you can make harmony with your psyche and uncover your real strength.

Extravagance is yielding to outrage, lethargy, habit, or overeating. It can likewise come from a position of bashing yourself for coming up short or not achieving an objective. Extravagance can mean being thankless.

A considerable lot of life's issues come from our absence of poise. Luckily, you can kick out that propensity by developing order through reflection. Reflection frees your brain from the dirtiness of guilty pleasure and interruption—much like tidying up a filthy room. On the off chance that you tidy up a room every day, you rule out the earth to settle. In any case, when you leave a room unswept, even a perfect one, dust settles, and over the long haul, this residue turns out to be thick and upsetting. Day by day, contemplation clarifies your psyche and soul little by little every day, eliminating modest residue quantities before they become troublesome for your self-control.

Contemplation places yourself in the now. It centers around the essential things and drives away pointless concerns. A thoughtful person is tolerant of their circumstances. What's more, through development and quietness, such a psyche is likewise dedicated to development.

Tranquility allows you to discover the reality. Simply make a stride back and relax. Allow your emotions to come and go. Invest time every day to clear the room that is your psyche.

Quite possibly, the best technique for self-restraint is through contemplation. With reflection, you can break free from fixation, improve mindfulness and discover harmony, which are central parts of settling on gainful choices.

Harmony is installed somewhere inside us—more profound than our outer interruptions. Unwind and resist the urge to panic, and harmony would move through each cell in your body. By thinking consistently, you can access internal harmony and locate a genuine concentration. Contemplation is fit for dissolving each mass of uncertainty, opening up and extending space for development in your heart. With day-by-day reflection, you can discover a route around your feelings of dread and tap into that inward quietness and satisfaction that stream from the well of confidence.

Contemplating works. Fast morning reflection will keep your brain prepared and adjusted for the day ahead. Reflection gives you that loosening up inclination equipped for launching your day to improve things. It is tied in with ruminating pretty much all you appreciate for a while, giving yourself some sure push.

Chapter 22: How to Seduce Women?

You are presumably similar to numerous men out there on the off chance you picked this book. You experience difficulty and fear regarding winning ladies, particularly regarding being a tease and attempting to get her into bed. It's a typical issue for men, and only a few men are whizzes in regard to appeal and enchantment. In any case, it doesn't mean you can't succeed in regard to winning ladies.

Certainty is necessary concerning ladies. It is a love potion to ladies. Ladies can identify certainty since it is the thing that they search for in a man. Dating has become an enemy of men's certainty. You may even think that it's challenging to ask a lady out on a date. You may ponder:

- How would you get yourself to take that action?
- How would you look at her straight without flinching and make your solicitation?

From numerous points of view, the capacity to have command over sex and affection characterizes what your identity is. The capacity to win women improves your interior satisfaction and self-esteem. When you prevail regarding winning ladies, you will receive the rewards of your manly aspiration and trust in your capacities. This will subsequently support your self-assurance.

What you need to know is how to increase your odds of winning a lady. Here are twelve techniques that can kick you off, with sights set on prevailing upon a sentimental possibility:

Be Committed to the Cause

Here you should make a committed move to prevail upon her, regardless of whether the reaction is adverse. You should continue asking ladies out and isolate yourself from the negative results. Try not to accuse yourself or peer down on yourself when the appropriate response is consistently negative after a few preliminaries. It can take you longer than a year to get the ultimate date. You should simply remain focused on the course, and on the off chance that one lady isn't intrigued, you will ultimately discover a match who is ideal for you.

Know Yourself

Here you ought to set up whether you are gay, indiscriminate, straight, or not distinguished by any means. You should figure out which side you are on and acknowledge what your identity is. At the point when you know and acknowledge yourself, you will collaborate effectively with others. Figuring out how to discuss proficiently with women and getting them to like you will help you accomplish your fearlessness target. You should be the sort of individual you need to pull in.

Be Yourself

After you have known yourself and acknowledged yourself, you should simply act naturally. Try not to battle to be another person; it's challenging to keep up a fake personality. Never give her a false impression of what your identity is, or act like you can't keep up. Women will succumb to you on the off chance that you don't overstate your capacities by striving hard to dazzle them instead of being genuine.

Gain Confidence Before Approaching Her

In winning ladies, you will consistently find that those men who are confident are more effective. This has nothing to do with the best of luck.

Ladies incline toward you to be a sure individual—not easygoing and uncertain of yourself. Ladies don't care for men who stand unapproachable and take a gander at them furtively. Whether it is for a single night rendezvous or long haul, ladies won't think about dating a washout.

You need the certainty to move toward ladies. When you realize how to converse with ladies and have the correct demeanor, you will begin to radiate confidence. With more certainty and a lot of training, you will find that this book's methods can help you connect with any lady you want.

Keep Practicing

Continuously practice and practice—over and over. Probably the greatest mix-up that you can make in this undertaking is to begin by conversing with the most delightful lady in the room.

On the off chance that you are not used to doing this, you will begin questioning yourself. Consequently, the inconvenience will start here because you will immediately rationalize why you can't move toward somebody. These questions emerge because you haven't put resources into chatting with numerous ladies to be adequately sure to move toward the one that you have indeed begun to be starrily eyed at.

Accordingly, similar to any area throughout everyday life, persistent practice will help you fantastically. You will fabricate your certainty gradually and start having discussions with ladies—only talking without any assumptions. This incorporates individuals you are not pulled in to.

When you practice tenaciously, your certainty will develop, and it will be simpler to begin discussions with arbitrary ladies. With time, you will have no issue strolling across that packed room and picking the lovely woman who has pulled in you.

Pick a Good Dating Location

Another incredible tip to help you meet the sort of ladies you want that make it simpler to chat with them is to pick a kind of scene that causes you to feel comfortable. Maybe you don't care for the bar or club scene, for instance. This could make moving toward ladies in these areas more troublesome on the off chance that you scorn hollering over the music or seeming as though a bonehead on the dance floor—except if you realize how to move.

Rather than utilizing that as a way to meet ladies, think about classes, such as a craft class or a cooking class, heading to the recreation center, a rancher's market or supermarket, or an exhibition hall. Discover those areas that you appreciate, and you will find that you are more agreeable and sure about moving toward ladies and chatting with them.

Always Keep Learning

Building your certainty is a vital starting advance. You can generally learn new things like being interested and open to new encounters, and continuous learning are vital.

Be Humorous, Hygienic, and Always Smile

These are fundamental perspectives for you to create before hitting on a woman. But you still need to get out there and meet ladies who will be keen on you and who will need to lay down with you. Regardless of how much and long you talk, you won't go anyplace with her on the off chance that you are humorless, blunt, and cleanliness testing. Consider the big picture from the lady's point of view for a touch. Would you want to return home with a woman who doesn't care for herself and who was inauspicious more often than not? Likely not.

That is the reason this part is tied in with chipping away at yourself and making yourself into a fair catch before you fire attempting to connect with ladies. By making these strides now and making a few improvements in your day-to-day life, you will find that it can help you build the certainty talked about in this book—you will be more joyful with your identity and what you have to bring to the table.

You will radiate certainty, and that is the thing that such countless ladies find alluring, regardless of whether they are searching for a single night rendezvous or somebody with whom they can fabricate a genuine relationship.

Improve Your Overall Physical Appearance

We're not looking at running out and getting the plastic medical procedures to look like whoever the current heartbreaker entertainer or artist is at present. It's undeniably more precise than that—luckily. You will locate that regardless of whether you are an ordinary person or maybe even not precisely an average person, you can do many things to help change and improve your actual appearance to make you more appealing.

Keep Fit

Keeping fit is a crucial part of improving your certainty and having the lady you had always wanted. The initial step is to ensure that you are taking adequate consideration of yourself regarding your general well-being. In addition to the fact that it is fundamental for your well-being, it is urgent to how ladies see you. You can be confident that they need something comparable from the men they pick—on the off chance you plan to lay down with attractive ladies with delightful bodies.

Whether you are overweight, fat, or only skin, bones, and a smidgen of muscle, you can improve. On the off chance that you have a few assets, invest some cash and energy in shedding a few pounds and building muscle. You don't have to have a six-pack or you don't have to look like a top model, but you need to ensure you are fit as a fiddle and that you look great.

For some men, the journey to fitness may be more extended than it is for others. Maybe you've dismissed dealing with yourself for some time now, or perhaps fitness was never necessary to you. Right now, is an ideal opportunity to begin getting into an extraordinary shape. You will feel good and look better too. At the point when this occurs, you will be overflowing with energy and certainty.

How to get fit is going to rely upon how you wish to look or the body you want to have, regardless of whether you are attempting to get in shape or assemble your muscles. A few men might be thin and might need to add a few muscles. To accomplish this, you can go to the rec center if you have a reasonable one in your general vicinity. You can likewise think about climbing, swimming, strolling, or running. You need not spend a great deal of cash to get into a great. Workout and bodyweight activities can change your life.

This book's objective isn't to give you a lot of exercise routines to show you how to workout. All things being equal, it will show you how to single out associations with ladies. Getting into shape is only one of the viewpoints you should consider.

Ensure you finish the proposed practice plan and put in the vital energy and exertion needed to get into shape before you start attempting to swagger around a club trying to get ladies. The better shape you are in, the simpler it will be to win ladies.

Dress to Impress

Notwithstanding getting your body into shape, you need to consider different parts of your outward appearance. This unquestionably includes the garments and shoes that you are wearing.

Individuals state that you ought never to pass judgment flippantly. In any case, it's human instinct to do precisely that. Individuals judge dependent on appearances, and there's no way around that. If you somehow happened to see an available lady in battered, grimy warm-up pants, wearing an old loose shirt and a cigarette hanging out of her mouth, you are likely not going to believe she's the most appealing lady in the room.

Chapter 23: Being a Leader Is a Good Thing

Effective leadership can be nerve-wracking. Being an effective leader to a team of people counting on you and inspire them to steer them in the right direction to achieve a common goal is an even more overwhelming task.

It's a lot of responsibility, but a real leader can effectively manage their team and bring out the best in everyone under their guidance.

A successful leader is one that can bring out the best in everyone that they work with. They are the ones who know how to spearhead the journey to success.

A great leader has a healthy mix of several qualities that contribute to their overall success, among which include:

Being Honest and Acting with Integrity

In the wise words of Dwight D. Eisenhower, the 34th President of the United States, "Leadership's supreme quality is unquestionably integrity. Without it, real success is not possible."

No matter which leadership position you hold, whether in a company, a sports team, an army, or any scenario in which you're in charge of a group of people, you will never achieve real success without integrity and honesty.

You must demonstrate the ability to stand by your core values and beliefs, and only when your followers see that they can place their trust in you will they become confident in your leadership abilities.

Being Confident

Before you can lead others, you need to be confident enough in your ability to do so.

Other people will not follow your leadership and commands if you are not sure about your decisions.

No one is going to believe in a leader who's always nervous and second-guessing their own decisions.

An effective leader always needs to display both confidence and assertiveness—a strength that others can take comfort in.

Be Respectful Towards Everyone

Respect is one of the vital critical principles that absolutely must be present, as a leader must respect their subordinates to gain respect in return. Respect, however, needs to be earned and never demanded.

When leaders don't respect their followers and vice versa, things can unravel quickly—and not in a positive way.

The best type of leaders and managers are the ones that provide a work environment where employees help each other and value the contributions that everyone makes.

An effective leader always encourages and helps their followers overcome challenges they face without belittling them.

Being an Inspiration

Being inspirational is probably one of the more challenging leadership tasks you could take on.

You need to set a good example yourself if you want others to follow in your lead.

As the leader, all eyes will always be on you and how you handle difficult situations.

As the 6th President of the United States, John Quincy Adams once said, "You're a leader if your actions inspire others to learn more, dream more, become more, and do more."

The ability to stay calm and composed under pressure, remain optimistic when others can't, think positively, and solve problems creatively is that's what constitutes an effective leader.

Consistency Is Key

One of the worst things you could do as a leader is to appear disorganized and scattered.

As a leader, you need to remember that everyone is looking to you for guidance, and it is you that they take their orders from.

To be effective, you must be consistent in the way you do things. Be fair in your treatment and your rewards. Be consistent in your methods of leadership and be consistent in your principles.

Be Passionate and Committed

People will be looking at you to guide them, and they're not going to be motivated to do their best if their leader doesn't display the same passion and commitment towards achieving that goal.

When a leader is not afraid to roll up their sleeves and get their hands dirty too, others will follow them because of the commitment and the passion for getting the job done that is being demonstrated.

That is how to earn the respect of your subordinates. Without commitment and passion, it's going to be an uphill task for any leader to keep the motivational fire going.

Be an Example

An effective leader is someone who can lead by example. Practice what you preach because your people are watching you and what you do. If you insist on your team being punctual, you need to ensure that you are punctual. If you remain calm and relaxed in stressful situations, your team will do the same.

Be someone that your team can look up to and respect, and show them the right thing to do by doing it yourself first.

Exhibit Good Communication Skills

A leader needs to have excellent communication skills to work with, or it's going to be very hard to explain your vision and tell them what needs to be done to accomplish a goal.

It will be a struggle to get the results you want if you can't demonstrate practical communication abilities.

Words have the power to inspire, motivate—and make people push past their boundaries—accomplishing things that they never thought were possible.

When a good leader uses the power of good communication skills, there's no limit to what they can inspire their team to accomplish.

Exhibit Decision-Making Abilities

As the one in charge, making decisions is going to be part of your leadership responsibilities.

You must demonstrate the ability to make the right decisions when the time calls for it—and this is no easy feat.

Every choice you make has a consequence and an impact on you and the people under your leadership.

You must think carefully about every decision you want to make because once the wheels are in motion, you're going to have to stand by your choice.

If there's a lot at stake, it might be best to get others' opinions who have a significant stake in the decision.

Be Accountable

You're accountable for what you and your subordinates do.

When they struggle, you struggle along with them, and when they succeed, give them the credit and acknowledgment that they deserve for a job well done.

If they stumble, work with them to see how you can all improve.

Be Willing to Listen

A leader needs to be a good listener and not just listen for the sake of doing so.

You need to be able to listen actively and pay attention to what your team has to say.

You are the one they will go to when they feel something needs to be improved. When your people feel that their leader is taking their every concern seriously, no matter how small it may be, and is taking steps to fix it, they will feel appreciated and acknowledged, which eventually spur them on to work better and perform better.

Be Innovative and Creative

Innovation and creativity are what distinguishes a leader from a follower.

In today's ever-changing world, it's not enough to be just one or the other anymore. A great leader needs to have both these qualities to think outside the box when others can't and turn ideas into reality. That's what makes them a leader, not a follower.

Have Empathy

A leader that chooses to go with the dictatorial approach to leadership may get things done, but that doesn't necessarily make them a great leader.

A leader can never make the meaningful connections they need to if empathy is not present.

Being an effective leader means you need to be able to put yourself in your team's shoes, and by understanding their concerns, you're one step closer to making a difference in their lives and performance.

That's how you become a great leader.

Developing Emotional Intelligence as a Leader

In most contexts, it is reasonably easy to determine who the leader is—at home, at work, among friends, in the classroom, in organizations (even the volunteer ones), even politicians.

Some specific individuals stand out and usually establish themselves as the one who oversees everyone else.

They have vision, charisma, goals, and problem-solving capabilities and strategies.

But of course, that alone is not enough. Emotional intelligence (EI) must be present too.

Emotional intelligence is a necessary part of leadership because it helps a leader to adapt and change when they need to—even at the last minute.

The ability to navigate others' emotions (and themselves) will help them manage the unexpected twists and turns that life might throw at them.

To become the effective leader that you want to be, you must work on improving EI skills, which means that you need to:

Make Self-Awareness a Priority

It is the only way you're going to learn how to grow from the experiences (and mistakes) of the past and guarantee the success of your future endeavors.

Broaden the Way You View the World

One of the biggest mistakes you could make as a leader would be to confine your circle to only people who talk, act, speak and look like you do.

An effective leader with a broader view of the world develops the ability to see things from multiple points of view, making better, informed decisions to ensure the best possible outcome.

In a world that is increasingly becoming more globalized, a leader needs to be open-minded now more than ever.

Create a Sense of Security

Your followers need to feel comfortable enough to be able to voice their opinions and concerns.

Suppose they are having difficulty working with another member of their team. In that case, they need to feel comfortable enough to approach you, the leader and bring up those concerns without worrying that there will be repercussions for themselves.

As a leader, you need to establish yourself as a trustworthy figure and encourage an open-door policy among the people you are managing, encouraging them and making them feel safe whenever they approach you with a problem.

Recognize Differences

To be an effective leader that solves problems for good so that it doesn't keep recurring, you need to tailor your solutions depending on the person you are dealing with.

If person A comes to you with a problem, when they walk out your office door, make sure it is with a solution that is perfect for the situation they are going through.

And when person B comes to see you, do not give them the same solution you gave person A.

Although these two people may face a similar problem, the way they approach or handle the problem will differ because they are two different personalities.

The problem will be perceived differently and, as such, affect them differently in the process.

Treat the individuals in your team as precisely what they are, individuals.

Enhance Your Inner Strength

In your leadership, there are going to be moments that push you beyond your limits. Moments that challenge you and threaten to defeat you and test your will to see what you're made of.

For this reason, you must develop inner strength as part of your overall EI skills to still exhibit self-control and positivity despite the difficulties faced.

Cultivate a Nurturing Nature

An effective leader is not afraid of a challenge, even if the challenge comes from working with someone who may be smarter than they are.

Chapter 24: How to Handle Jealousy?

What Does Envy in a Relationship?

At the root of envy exists the stress of misfortune. Like loads of jealous colleagues, Kevin suffered from a deficiency in his relationships, lack of confidence, and lack of faith. Has very anxious and envious. Those things made him be very frail—he was also treated like a moron by his friends because of that.

Envy brings about sensations more intense than a feeling of dread; for example, rage, disdain of 'adversaries,' disturbance (infrequently self-appall), and misery.

So, for what reason may an individual be envious? Kevin's ex had ripped off on him, and he believed he'd never deserved this. He was sometimes assaulting himself and didn't realize the danger he was doing to himself. He was educated and had an extraordinary, creative mind; nonetheless, he was using that to torment himself. Obviously, on the off chance that your accomplice is frequently explicitly lively with others, and at that point, desire is aroused in others, and then your relationship might have troubles

In any case, here I expect to focus on encouraging you if you feel unduly desirous (that is to guarantee, there is no genuine or right verification that your friend is or has deceived you). These tips additionally center around sex-related envy instead of being envious of the measure of time your buddy goes through with their mother or youths. So precisely, how might we start to harm the desired cycle, recuperate self-limitation, and drive our friends and ourselves insane?

If you are in an ongoing relationship, it is normal to feel somewhat desirous on occasion—explicitly if you have solid affections for your love partner. Intermittent jealousy is alright and may even incorporate a little enthusiasm and zing to the relationship. But what to do when the sensation that others desire your partner becomes more intense and continuous?

For What Reason Do People Get Jealous?

The more reasonable and logical explanation for jealousy is that guys dread sex-related cheating as they need to be sure that their posterity is theirs. Females are significantly more keen on enthusiastic extramarital relations since they are keen on their adolescents' endurance and wish to make sure that their partners underpin their children and shield them.

Today like never before, people fear being dismissed, declined, not being adored, and wasting time with the people have romantic or sexual interactions with. These sensations of misfortune are all-common. However, when accepted, just as envy's sensations are extreme, they stem mostly from weaknesses. On the off chance that you experience jealousy regularly, below are a few methods that will help you out:

Try Not to Act Upon Your Sensations

It is troublesome not to act upon the things you are feeling. The sensation of desire or some other sensations isn't the issue; the actual trouble starts when you begin working upon that envy and let it burn through you. You can feel jealous but don't need to follow up on it. Recall that your mate is a person that is effectively speaking about her surroundings. There may be many men wanting to have sex with your partner, but that doesn't mean they will have a go with her behind your back. Remember that there is an explanation as to why she stays in a personal relationship with you. If she wanted to date other men, no doubt, they would. Along these lines, whenever you feel envious, favor the sensations, yet change the strategy and you think about the situation and be sensible as well as reasonable.

Quiet Down and Remain Vulnerable

To appreciate is to be vulnerable. George R.R. Martin expressed it delightfully, he said, "The more individuals you cherish, the more fragile you will be." What you ought to do is hold nothing back from your partner, or display jealousy-related outbursts, and avoid panicking. Indeed, it is testing, yet you need to be glad to endorse what is past your control and trust her about your doubts. Remember, you stay in the relationship since you choose to appreciate it. It is a decision you make to love your partner and, simultaneously, support her without jelousy-related situations.

Express Your Jealousy in a Soft Method

If you feel that your partner is accomplishing something that is making you jealous, you can share precisely how you feel, just talk with her and gradually imply your concern. You can similarly include touching her tactfully or say it straight as long as it is chivalrous. If you are entertaining, you can joke concerning precisely how surprisingly jealous you are when she goes all about another person. Try to smile and laugh while you express your concern because doing so will ease the heat off the point and get the message all through. When you are conciliatory, you can allow her to comprehend that you like her a ton and realize that she can never betray you. What's more, on the off chance that you want to say straight, basically tell her that you trust her no matter what but cannot deal with your sentiments and want her to consider exactly how you feel.

Worth Yourself

Among the fundamental reasons why individuals get jealous is that they have low confidence and uncertainty issues. In general, they will feel that they are unacceptable; their buddy will surely get this and leave them for another person. You need to perceive that there is an explanation that your accomplice loved you in any case and even got along with you. On the off chance that you need some reaffirmation or thankfulness, don't reconsider to request that as well (sensibly speaking, obviously). Whenever you feel jealous, remember that your buddy is with you since they plan to be with you due to your ideal characteristics.

Recuperate Your Injuries

Individuals regularly will, in general, act out of jealousy in light of past associations too. You may have been harmed before, just as they might have ripped off on you. You need to move past your past and understand that you moved on from those terrible relationships and now you are with luckily wit her—and she is not your ex. Understanding the roots, causes, and purposes behind your envy is a fundamental piece of personal development and saving a relationship. At whatever point you begin feeling envious,

196

put forth a conscious attempt to recuperate your old injuries. Be much more impervious to guarantee that your past doesn't impact your current and future.

Trust Your Lady

You should confide in your lady since you have no other decision if you need to have a pleased and dynamic relationship. Nobody is going to take your woman from you, and you need to let your jealousy go. Having some control is anything but a negative point, yet endeavoring to oversee someone for things you have no control is dangerous. Act affectionately regardless of the moments of jealousy you may experience.

Trust Yourself

The best thing that you can do is trust yourself. Trust yourself that you can cherish profoundly—without any second thoughts. Trust that your affection will act like the anchor that will dodge your relationship from coasting endlessly. This is troublesome, yet when you trust yourself, you trust her no matter what. You feel the certainty that you are saving her and yourself from dealing with possibly the most testing circumstances—a separation or disavowal.

At last, envy might be dangerous because infiltrates as a toxin in a relationship. If you follow the above tips just as techniques when feeling jealous, you will, without a doubt, stay in a better arrangement to build up your relationship and become and also become an alpha male.

Jealousy Turns into Outrage

Now you should know how to do so. This book may help cover a few gaps regarding how the brain turns understanding into self-judgment and diminished confidence into weakness. This book may help you acknowledge and change the way you live. In any case, to genuinely make effective changes, you will require an alternate range of abilities. Perceiving exactly how you produce your jealousy-fueled reactions doesn't give you adequate data about exactly how to change them. Much like changing a flat tire, you don't have a sense of victory when you have just removed the flat one, you have to mount the new tire now.

For the image, I'll utilize a man as a jealous person. I allude to various mental pictures.

It begins with a person's sensation of uncertainty concerning himself. Weakness begins from his "false hidden image" of being 'unacceptable.' With the conviction that he is a weak, unconfident and jealous person rather than it being just an image in his brain, the man produces self-dismissal in his psyche. The mental aftereffect of being self-dismissed is a vibe of shamefulness, flimsiness, worry, and hopelessness.

To get over the inclination made from his false hidden image, he focuses on his apparent positive characteristics. From these characteristics, the man builds up an extra great false image of himself. I call this the "projected picture" since this is precisely how he needs to be seen. The passionate result of a great self-image is no abstemiousness or vibe of dishonor. There is a higher acknowledgment for himself. In this way, he gives more love and is more blissful. Notice that he has not adjusted. He is merely clinging to different images in his psyche depending on the occasion.

The hidden image thoughts come to be the triggers of grief, while the projected image enacts much more lovely emotions. It is necessary to recall that the two pictures are false. The two pictures are in the man's brain and neither of them is him himself. He is the one that is making them up as he is reacting to the pictures in his inventive and creative mind. He isn't a picture in his creative vision.

The man's psyche connects the projected photo with the high characteristic women are acquired. Regularly the characteristics are viewed as significant because of the supposition that ladies are brought into his mind. When the man stands out enough to be noticed by a lady, the characteristics that woman require in a man into the projected picture rather than the "not good enough" picture. The projected picture's reinforced thought brings about more self-acknowledgment, love, and bliss in his imaginative experience.

It is the capacity of enacting and endorsement that changes his mood in the imaginative exercise, and not just the woman's being there in his mind. These changes in his mood also cause other changes in the thoughts he has that enable him to self-acknowledgment and self-love.

Conclusion

A true alpha does not have to prove anything to anybody. Watch one in action. He will be the one whom everyone looks up to. Someone who doesn't pick fights voluntarily but does not back down from them. Someone who holds his ground till the end of the battle. He doesn't go on about his conquests or wealth or the number of business deals he has clinched. He has class and knows how to display it so. Alphas do not throw their tongues around. They know exactly what attracts women to them—and it's not all about money. A true alpha is super confident, subtly assertive, cool, calm, and collected in all situations. No showing off at all. They know people will be attracted to their personalities.

Alphas are natural leaders. Whether we admit it or not, all of us are drawn to someone who can lead us as a cohesive group. Leaders are charismatic people who keep the group as one. This kind of confidence that alphas have gives them an extra inner strength to work with, which is all the more irresistible.

Now that you've learned about what being an alpha male is all about, it's time to master some alpha male traits and qualities. Here's a list to help you out:

- Be confident in your appearance and personality. Be proud of who you are, inside and out. If you're a man with a mean, gruff exterior, then be proud to be that kind of man. Confidence is sexy. Women want to be around a man with confidence.

- Be unambiguously masculine. Don't be wishy-washy with your personality. Be a man. Show her who's in charge.

- Know what you want. A confident man with a goal will eventually achieve it. If you want a woman, ask for her number. If you want sex, make it happen. If you want to get that job, work hard and get it. It's as simple as that. Alpha males don't rely on others to make their lives better. They are men in charge of their own lives—one way or another. A true alpha never has a problem using his alpha sexual charm to get what he wants.

- Own your power. If you're the boss, then make the rules and be the boss. Be the strongest, smartest, most dominant, and most successful boss ever. Be the most confident. Embrace your power and use it to your advantage.

- Show the world what a real alpha is. Use your body as a weapon—show her who is boss by showing off your massive sexual prowess. Women are attracted to a man who knows what he wants sexually and isn't afraid to express it.

- Be alpha in your work. Word on the street is that alphas are seen as comically macho in their professions. Avoid that. Present yourself in the most professional manner possible. A man with little confidence may choose to hide his inner alpha male some of the time. A true alpha male never hides. Alphas know that confidently displaying their sexuality and sexual prowess is the best way to win others' respect without giving power away.

- Be decisive and confident. We want to be surrounded by leaders because that's what true alphas are. Leaders need to make decisions quickly and confidently. Getting too stuck on the details can be a deal-breaker. If you are indecisive at any point in the decision-making process, she will feel the same way.

- Be decisive in what you do. If you purchase a new car, then go ahead and buy a new car. There's no need to twiddling around with your purchase. Live your life on a cliff's edge with no way to go back.

- Be cool, calm, and collected. There's a difference between confident and cocky. When you're confident, you can handle other people. Confident people attract others.

When you're too cocky, you can be disdained by other people.

- Be calm and confident. Show your confidence at all times.
- Always maintain control. This is the alpha male way of acting.
- Always be in control and know what you are doing. Be decisive and make a decision quickly, no matter how hard the decision is. If you lose control, you are going to lose everything you have. So never give up and think that you will fail somewhere.
- Realize that women love good-looking men, but beautiful women love men who like themselves. You've heard it all your life. It is an absolute fact that women love men who like themselves. That's why gorgeous men and ugly men still get the ladies. So, focus first on your looks and then on your personality. That's the best way to get a woman to love you.
- Don't shove your attractiveness down anyone's throat. You don't want to be known for no reason at all. Your attractiveness will be noticed if you are confident and if you are doing your job right. If you are going out with friends for a wild night out, there should be no chance anyone will leave you out.

- Keep a fast pace. If you don't, you'll lose girls' interest, but you will also lose your friends' respect.
- Surround yourself with people that you admire.
- Have a few weaknesses. This will make others respect you so much more.
- Don't get involved in wild parties. Trust me, it's fun to have a few drinks once in a while, but don't ever make wild parties a habit.
- Spend more time with your friends and family. When you're single, make sure you are still committed to your friends and family. Many men don't do that, but a true alpha is a man committed to his wife, girlfriend, friends, and family.
- Never stop believing in yourself.
- Thrive under adversity. The stronger the opposition, the healthier you are.
- Spin positives. If you fail at something such as a business deal, look for the positives in it and move forward.
- Never show desperation or emotion. Keep yourself under control at all times.
- Maintain integrity. Never, and I mean never, betray a friend.
- Don't ever let your guard down. You can never really trust anyone.

- Show emotional restraint. Keep your personal and private life private by any means necessary.
- Don't lie unless it's necessary.
- Don't ever, ever, tolerate anyone disrespecting you.
- Be true to yourself.
- Take control of your life.